July, 2018

Betty,
The presence of the Divine makes all the difference in the story of our lives.
　　　　Blessings,
　　　　Virginia Lynn

A Portrait in Progress

VIRGINIA LYNN

outskirts
press

A Portrait in Progress
All Rights Reserved.
Copyright © 2018 Virginia Lynn
v8.0

The opinions expressed in this manuscript are solely the opinions of the author and do not represent the opinions or thoughts of the publisher. The author has represented and warranted full ownership and/or legal right to publish all the materials in this book.

This book may not be reproduced, transmitted, or stored in whole or in part by any means, including graphic, electronic, or mechanical without the express written consent of the publisher except in the case of brief quotations embodied in critical articles and reviews.

Outskirts Press, Inc.
http://www.outskirtspress.com

ISBN: 978-1-4787-8824-9

Cover Photo © 2018 thinkstockphotos.com. All rights reserved - used with permission.

Outskirts Press and the "OP" logo are trademarks belonging to Outskirts Press, Inc.

PRINTED IN THE UNITED STATES OF AMERICA

Table of Contents

The Sketch 1
The Canvas: Prenatal Influence of My Birth Parents 5
The Background of My Adoptive Parents. 14
The Priming—Early Childhood 19
Nursing/Midwifery/Theological College 32
Liberian Years of Ministry 51
The Wainwright Saga 71
A Career-Wise Shift 101
Marriage to Kenneth 113
Finding My Genetic Background 123
Employment Termination 138
The Retreat at AL-VI-NOR 153
Investment ---Identity Capital 163
The Frame: Summation and Perspective 189

DEDICATION

To all my families---genetic, nuclear and extended. Your love and acceptance have helped mould me into the person God designed me to become. Designated love and blessings to you forever.

The Sketch

DEFINITION--a vague outline which promises more to come. Look for greater fullness, fine detailing and noteworthy texture.

ART INSTRUCTORS IN the human form often send out a call for real models. Young, female, male, aged, imperfect. All may apply if willing to be studied naked in unassuming positions. In the end only the intrepid should sign-up!

Naked models—interesting subject conversation. Especially individuals with withered bodies (perhaps *weathered* is a kinder adjective). Willingness to hold a specific pose for a determined length of time in front of youthful aspirants takes- -is there a better term?-- spunk. Write that in red capitals, please.

One hopes that those beginning an artistic career would be non-judgmental in attitude. It is what it is.

Nakedness implies "openness". Some private areas are occasionally and modestly hidden. Often times the artist must use imagination as a creative tool. Different sessions call for a variety of techniques. Ever see a hairy armpit sketched? Rare indeed.

The purpose of such a venture is to teach-without touching the intricacies of the divinely created human form. The original architectural design was perfect. Advancing years modify a body into something more complex and worthy of study.

Every newborn comes into this earth existence pure and innocent, aching to be loved and deserving of joyful cries at his/her appearance.

A sketch does not languish because it is not an exact replicate of a page out of *"Gray's Anatomy"* textbook for medical students. The ability to "expose" without creating an "exposé" is an art in itself.

Portraiture requires patience. Every face has a voice. Each individual has a story. The background adds a dimension and depth which needs to be told. Throw in a bit of intriguing information heretofore unknown and the picture becomes mysteriously unique.

In portrait painting a sketch is the preliminary step. The artist decides on a pose, an angle or a perspective that will guide her hands throughout the duration of the painting. Efforts to be true to that first impression will be painstakingly followed. Alterations for greater clarity are always encouraged.

Researching these stories was more than a trip down dimly lit pathways. It was in every way an odyssey into forgotten avenues and surprising recesses of memory. Every diary page, all the journal entries provided foder for recall excursions. Some good, others funny. All revealing.

The malodorous whiff which assaulted my nose when I opened boxes of letters and memorabilia from Liberia was...overpowering! Mildew DOES NOT improve with age. Stuffed into one yellowed manilla folder were samples of cloth and simple drawings of outfits sent to my adoptive mother (a seamstress) to show her what I was busy stitching into my wardrobe.

Reading the poignant letters ("Mummy, when are you and Daddy coming to get us?") from our sons immersed in an American missionary boarding school 360 miles away (it seems much longer in kilometers!) brought unheralded mistiness to my eyes. So glad that agonizing decision is a non-repeater. Pity the dear parents into whose lap that determination must land.

At times the house was airbrushed with the sounds of African music, the very atmophere vibrating with lively rhythms of handmade drums. Sitting in a comfy sofa-chair listening to my adoptive father's favorite music (Tchaikovshy's Nutcracker Suite), memories of Mom's fruitcake, African palm butter, freshly brewed *chai tea* effervescing, my recall became almost palpable.

My mother diligently kept every letter I wrote her during our sojourn in Liberia. Because fatigue was a constant bedfellow, many vignettes did not get recorded in an accessible place in my cranium. Reading about the childrens antics evoked a great deal of joy belonging to a time past. It was a case of full-flight reminiscence.

I am aware that my present reality is the accumulative result of my past experiences. As an emerging artist I decided the metaphor of a painting was an appropriate metaphor. It was a fortuitous moment when, on a recent visit to KingsFold Retreat near Cochrane, Alberta, I came upon the following quote by Francis Schaefer, artistically presented as a poster.

> *No work of art is more important than the Christian's own life. Every Christian is called upon to be an artist in this way. (S)he may have the gift of writing, the gift of composing or singing, but each (wo)man has the gift of creativity in terms of the way (s)he lives his/her life. In this sense, the Christian's life is to be a thing of truth and also a thing of beauty in the midst of a lost and despairing world.*

Everyone has a backstory. This crazy-busy world of technology with its bruising mindset, tempts all of us to judge before knowing all the fine details that soften the heart's response to any given situation. The end result of this endeavour is to illuminate family, friends and colleagues who will perhaps be entertained in the process.

Advancing years have shifted the focus of my activities, but not the central core of my being. Grounded in the eternal love of God, the lens through which I view life, rests the delicate balance of Providence and Sovereignty. One's lifestory begins with the first gasp in the birthing room and continues forward until the final exhalation.

Throughout the course of these pages I shall develop the theme of painting by following the steps associated with the great Flemish painters in the early 1500s. As this memoir took form I began to view the canvas of my life in a fresh light.

One final brush stroke. The names of persons have been changed where personal embarrassment might be involved.

The Canvas: Prenatal Influence of My Birth Parents

EARLY FLEMISH PAINTERS began their masterpieces on supports of wood (oak, beech, lime, poplar—whatever was available) . Regardless of the species, all were prepared with utmost care. The most exquiste works were laboriously intricate. Multiple layers of paint were interspersed single thicknesses of glazes. Drying time between stages occasionally stretched into weeks. Tedious work, no matter how quickly it takes to record the process. Often inferior layers were scraped out by delicate instruments. Each picture generally required six to twelve months to complete.

The wooden support had to be resilient and strong enough to withstand the assaults of the artist's creativity. Over the centuries, tough canvas became the preferred medium.

In 1785 Mr. John Bice sailed from England, hoping to escape political and religious persecution. The insufferable conditions of his sea voyage did not destroy his dream of experiencing freedom in a new country—America. He settled in Pennsylvania and began a career as a millwright.

His legacy was a large clan of Bices who for the most part, remained loyal to the British crown. After the American Revolution, his descendents, three generations removed, traveled north to Ontario. These settlers became known as United Empire Loyalists. In reality they were displaced persons because of their participation in the losing side of the American Revolution. Because of their loyalty to England, they endured the loss of property and saw their land confiscated.

It is generally believed the family of Bices settled in the Niagara Pennisula. Records indicate a Mr. John Bice received 300 acres of homestead land, perhaps as a reward for coming to Canada and swelling the population!

Arthur Gordon Bice was born in 1897. He and Mary Elizabeth Allen produced ten children. Evelyn Lorraine , the eldest, was born in 1917 in Brockville, Ontario.

Ten years later the family decided the long trek west to homestead country in northern Alberta was worth the tears of farewell and the anxiety of the unknown. A brave decision considering the agony of disrupted life and inevitable change. The Peace Country welcomed them as they sank new roots into virgin soil. By the time Evelyn had celebrated her tenth birthday, her family had already experienced four infant/childhood deaths.

She grew up in a household ruled by a tough, continually grumpy father who allowed no nonsense from either his partner nor his offspring. Her father owned and ran a small country store in a frontier town known as Bolloy. The town is non-existent today for reasons that are not difficult to understand. The children were expected to carry a fair share of the work at home as well as in the store. No questions asked or sloth allowed. Strictness was part and parcel of Evelyn's Dutch Reformed upbringing.

In her late teens she fell in love with a gentleman who worked on the CPR rail line. One thing led to another. The mid 1930s weren't all that different from the twenty first century! The day came when she knew for certain she was carrying his child. Try to imagine the panic.

Cultural ambience in rural Alberta during the Great Depression frowned on babies born without the trappings of a wedding. Even then there were secret methods to terminate this unthinkable occurence. This was a rude interruption to an otherwise quiet, discreet life. Her value system, ingrained by biblical precepts and ecclesiastical hubris, did not consider this a viable option.

Can you hear the "tsk tsks" and see the eyes rolled heavenward in horror? It doesn't take a huge bolt of imagination!

Ignoring the temptation to bring harm to herself or the baby, Evelyn hid the pregnancy. She confided in no one and dressed in loose-fitting outfits which accomplished her purpose. Not a single soul suspected. An unbelievable amount of courage and grace must have given her the fortitude to travel those lonely nine months with an ever-growing secret tucked under her apron.

One cold day in February 1936, while clerking in her father's store, she went into labour. Summoning up her bravest face she excused herself. In a darkened storage room near the back of the establishment she delivered a baby boy. Think of the pain, physical as well as psychological. From all accounts it must have been what is termed "a precipitate birth".

Try to fathom the stunned reaction when she came out holding the infant swaddled in a towel she had grabbed from the nearby shelves. The dismay and shock quickly turned into white-hot rage. The new postpartum patient was now next to a newly disowned daughter. Somehow the rupture was sutured by humbleness and grace, although the wound remained fragile for decades to come.

The beginning of sorrows.

The new father became a "runaway daddy". The prospect of fatherly responsibilities was too much for him to bear. He sent his love a letter of farewell accompanied with a gift of $100, "to raise the baby" he wrote. I cannot condone his flight from responsibility, but my feelings are softened by the peace offering which at the time was a considerable amount. No further communication occurred in the years that transpired.

The baby was named Roy. In an ironic twist of fate he was introduced to his birth father at a convention of Jehovah Witnesses decades later. The older gentleman refused to acknowlege this son who appeared out of nowhere. It was as though the incident forty

A Portrait in Progress

years previous had never occured. This second rejection was a deeper trauma than the initial abandonment.

An unanswerable question begs to be asked--"*Did Evelyn ever meet him by chance somewhere along her life journey?*" I do not have the answer. She endured the ridicule of the family and community for a few months before fleeing to Edmonton where she found a measure of safety and peace.

Shortly after settling into her life as a single parent without support, visible or invisible, a man with a winning smile and true depth came marching into her sphere. His name was Joseph Aaron Green, an Ontarian by birth but transplanted into Alberta when his parents had relocated their family of eight children to Fort Saskatchewan in 1906. They homesteaded on farm land in the district of Sunnyside.

Young Joe had the gifting and urge to become a chef after leaving the family farm. A number of positions held his attention until he decided Edmonton was the best place to showcase his culinary skills.

Details of their romance are lamentably few. I have a copy of their wedding certifcate in my possession. They were married on May 6, 1936 in the parsonage of a clergyman named Rev. Gordon Skitch, an ordained minister with the Christian and Missionary Alliance church. Two witnesses signed the registry, Helen Erickson and Frances Skitch, wife of the officiant. Why no "best man" to stand with the groom?

The picture which calls forth tears is their wedding day. Two sober souls dressed in non-descript outfits. The bride is holding a baby wrapped in a white blanket,covering his little features. Taking on the resposibilies of feeding and caring for another man's child was a gesture of magnanimity. Evelyn was nineteen, her husband had already celebrated his thirty fifth natal day. The couple settled into the rhythm of matrimony in Edmonton.

Researching a history book about the town and surrounding area of Fort Saskatchewan gave me some interesting insights into the family dynamics of the Green household. What was omitted from the text was even more intriguing. In the precise detailing of all the births, marriages and deaths of John Robinson Green, patriarch of the family, the fact of Joe and Evelyn's union was a notable omission. His second marriage to Mary Calder and the family of 5 children is mentioned, however.

The little family resided in Edmomton where Joe was employed as a chef. Roy was an active, tow-headed two and a half year old youngster when baby Eileen made her appearance. Right from her first babble she was pale and lethargic. She was diagnosed as a "blue baby". A congenital heart defect prevented oxygen-rich blood from circulating throughout her body causing the skin to appear a bluish hue. Attending doctors told her parents she had "a hole in her heart". This was the era prior to open heart surgery and other life-saving technologies. The best advice the medical establishment could give the horror stricken parents was, *"Take the baby home and love her until she dies."*

Eileen lived eight months and then died in her mother's arms one dark evening. When Joe returned home and heard the news, he accused Evelyn of deliberately killing the baby. It was a horrible reaction to the keenest of all losses.

Shortly thereafter and understandable from this faraway perspective, the bonds of devotion began to disengage. It is now common knowledge that some couples in grief cannot cope with the loss of a child. They wrestle with the grief demons on different levels and bring to the process their inherent ways of dealing with crisis, frequently neglecting the care and nurturing of each other.

Deep sorrow is often laced with anger and blame tactics. It can escalate to monstrous heights if no intervention is available. In the midst of clamoring chaos, Evelyn became pregnant. Joe allegedly took the news as an opportunity to berate his wife for (in his view) the apparent lack of mothering skills. Threatening statements(*you can bear the baby, but I get to keep it*) become part of her day to day existence.

And so it came to pass, just before the church bells announced the dawning of the New Year 1941, a girl child was born in the labour and delivery ward of Edmonton's Royal Alexander Hospital. She was named Rosemary Diane. After the requisite ten day hospital stay, my broken-hearted mother kissed me good bye, walked out of the

A Portrait in Progress

hospital and away from her husband's angry presence. She and 5 year old Roy traveled back to Grande Prairie where she did her best to forget and rebuild.

She covenanted in her heart that no one would ever know the events of the preceeding four years. Not a word slipped out until sixty years later when the back story was met with utter disbelief. Did anyone ever ask her about the years of absence? Did Roy never ask a question out loud about what happened to Daddy? Why was Mommy so sad all the time?

My birth father picked me up from the nursery and found a gracious family to "foster" me while he continued working. God only knows what he told them surrounding the circumstances of my birth.

Divorce papers (I have a zeroxed copy tucked away in a special file) were signed on June 14, 1941. Interestingly enough, the application for the divorce was filed two weeks before I was born. The reason given for the marriage dissolution? Adultery, on the part of the defendant! *No* proof was required or provided. Do I want to dance with the skeletons in someone else's closet? I have chosen not to do so.

There was no further contact, either written or verbal, between my birth parents from that time onward, even though they had close mutual friends who could have supplied information had it been requested. Stories which have survived the intervening decades, but perhaps withered with rancor, suggest an affair with a brother-in-law. Before or after my birth---who cares? How does that affect my reality? Not too much.

Listening to older relatives on the Bice family tree and reading the history book account of the Green kindred with the absence of important details causes me to reflect on the cruelty of silence. What does this imply? My own visceral feeling is a great sadness that two entirely distinct family units could totally ignore three little people who were profoundly affected by this couple. Unexplainable circumstances beyond their reach turned them into "non personas" by two clans, without apparent remorse.

Reading Dr. Thomas Verny's *Parenting Your Unborn Child* and *The*

Secret Life of the Unborn Child years ago while developing an evening seminar for volunteers at a pregnancy care center gave me pause. Research on the relationships between spouses and parents shows that harmony positively correlates with an easy pregnancy and the birth of a healthy child. I wondered about the stress level precipitated by quarreling parents on a pre-born child. Did it adversely affect me? I have reason to believe while still cradled in Evelyn's womb, I heard them discussing my fate. More about that in a later chapter.

Quoting Dr.Verny-a baby *"has the ability to register and respond to her mother's thoughts, feelings and spoken words. Babies pick up on the emotional charge that all spoken language carries."*

Research has been conducted which provides data that an unborn child hears, recognizes his/her mother's voice, and here's the shocker, can remember the words!

The canvas was in place. The painting was about to proceed.

Joe and Evelyn Green, May 4, 1936

Norman and Alice Thompson, June 6, 1927.

The Background of My Adoptive Parents.

ROSCOMMON IS AN idyllic landlocked county in Eire (southern Ireland). It boasts of verdant hills, sheep aplenty, appalling curves on narrow roads and century-old ruins. All this minus crashing waves of either the Irish Sea or the Atlantic Ocean. An interpretive center detailing the horrors of the infamous potato famine sits on a lush prominence in Strokestown, a mere 30 kilometers away. An unforgettable experience awaits visitors who enter the doors of the building. It calls for sober reflection on the inhumanity forced upon citizens by an unengaged government.

Alexander Thompson was a member of the Royal Irish Constabulary. He and his wife, Mary Jane Beatty raised eight children during his tenure in the police force. Norman Ernest, the second youngest was born on December 13, 1897. His birthplace, as stated on his birth certificate, was a room in the local barracks.

His parents carried their new baby boy to a small Church of England chapel on January 11, 1898 for his christening ceremony. The sanctuary still stands today, its musty ambiance reminding us that even though the family was in the minority (5%) of the surrounding religious population, Roman Catholic, there existed a calm co-existence. I stood by the altar and read the feathery handwriting of the clergyman who duly noted that Norman Ernest was christened according to the ecclesiastical ritual required by the church. As a side note, I received a dispensation of grace by the rector in charge to play the ancient pump organ that no doubt was in place at the time of my father's christening. Moments like that are hallowed.

The family was devastated by the death of Mary Jane. Norman was twelve at the time. A tender note in her will (which presupposes a terminal or lingering disease as opposed to an accident) instructs Eveleen, the oldest sibling, to look after "dear little Norman".

Sometime in his mid or late teens he found his place in Dublin working at the Guinness Whiskey company. Such fun in those barrel rooms! Not much remuneration though. My favorite anecdote, always recounted with unabashed laughter was the time a derelict patron found his way into the distillery. His annoying presence soon got the better of the employees good humor. He asked for "a pint" and in their youthful mischief they gave him "a quart". The poor soul promptly sank into a deep faint, frightening the lads beyond measure. They pulled him out into the alley, propped him up against a brick wall and prayed for mercy should he die. A week later he strolled in, evidently none the worse for his escapade, and asked for another round like the last one!

On Easter Sunday 1916, rebels launched a bloody, ill-fated insurrection against their British overlords. It was quelled in six days, but the feeling of peace and safety never returned.

Seeking a brighter future with better prospects, the brave young gentleman set sail for Montreal with the equivalent of twenty dollars in his pocket. Relying on grit and good humour, he found his way to Winnipeg on a CPR train. A number of odd jobs kept body and soul together. Along the way he encountered signs for immediate employment, but with the coda, *No Irish need apply.* Sigh. Winnipeg offered a friendlier face .

Ahh-hh. Yes, it was different in Winnipeg. Perhaps because the legendary founder of Eaton's was an Irish-born entrepreneur with an outstanding reputation for fairness and marketing skill. Immediate employment was offered.

Eaton's Department Store, on Portage Avenue and Hargrave Street, offered him employment in the furniture department. For years excellent quality furniture became his passion. I have a couple of fine examples in my home that were purchased shortly after his marriage to Alice.

When Eaton's closed their doors in 1997 (bankruptcy!) it was a scathing commentary on the behavior of the founders quarrelsome descendants. I have a black blouse I purchased during the dying days of their existence as a proud Canadian company. It hangs in my closet to this day.

Alice Anderson's background was American. Born in Lightfoot, Virginia shortly after the emergence of the 20th century, all her forbears were of Norwegian or Swedish descent. When Alice, middle child of five, was a mere toddler, a decision was made to emigrate to Canada. All their worldly goods were securely packed in a covered wagon and off they set, ending up in an area called Clanwilliam, Manitoba. I ache for the details of that sojourn.

Her father had the opportunity to become a lay minister sanctioned by the Lutheran Church. His stamina served him well as he plowed, seeded and harvested on the homestead. Some years were unforgiving in their harshness.

Gramma Anderson won her way into the hearts of the nearby neighbours by her compassionate midwifery skills. She was called upon to attend many births, good weather as well as winter, often on horseback as no other means of transportation was easily available during those early years. No doubt the payment for her services came in the form of eggs, cream and occasionally bacon which eased the financial crunch of those pioneer days. I loved hearing her tell of the time she dropped a dead mouse into her grandfather's mouth as he snored his way to a restful respite. She hid under a bed once after ruining his pipe by accidentally perforating it while trying to clean out the ashes.

Alice "migrated" to Winnipeg sometime in her early twenties. The mail order department was an important part of the Eaton empire. Eaton's catalog became a Canadian icon. Merchandise from all over the world was stored in warehouses not far from the original building. Alice's employment was mostly spent in the drug and chemical area. Opening letters of request from across the country, sorting them into specific files, filling the orders and then packaging the goods on their way to buyers became part and parcel of her daily routine.

The company provided leisure activities along with health benefits and proper wages. Somewhere along the line, an invitation for a blind date introduced Alice to her future husband. They courted for three years before solemnizing their union in 1927 at St. Matthews Anglican Church . The Official Notice of Marriage (aka the marriage certificate) included two questions government of the time needed to know about the bride and her groom---could they both read and write? Not sure about the rationale of that inquiry. The handwritten signatures written on that special day were almost identical to the their handwriting just prior to their passing many years later.

Alice's wedding dress—a delicate teal-coloured silk frock with three ruffles at the hemline—hangs in an upstairs closet in my home. It was a quiet, happy household. Her entire family had been thrilled by the intense preaching of an evangelist, Rev. Watson Argue. She along with her siblings committed themselves to God during revival services in Winnipeg's Calvary Temple.

At the time of their wedding, Norman was unconvinced, but not adverse to regular church activities. Some time later he too committed his life to God. Weeks after his conversion, he was elected as a church board member. This type of responsibility followed him until the day he died. The latter few years of his life the designation was "elder".

By all accounts Norman and Alice were a very social couple. They had close friends with whom they enjoyed snow shoeing and spent time dining. A move to Calgary occurred a decade later. The reasons have been forgotten, unfortunately. They settled into a duplex across the street from a lady called Mrs. Luck. This spry woman organized Alberta's first Home and School Association, an institution which brought parents and teachers together with the good of the students as an uppermost goal. When she died, her antique Hammond piano came to live in our Edmonton home. I learned my piano lessons on that beautifully crafted instrument . In time I sold it to a close friend in Sylvan Lake whose kindness makes me teary every time I visit her. She lets me play it for old times sake.

Jonathan Stephenson wrote a text which included a chapter on the materials and techniques of the early Flemish masters. Here is what he wrote about the initial portion of a painting.

> ..*meticulous detail and numerous superimposed layers are required to produce subtle effects of shade and light..... It is essential to begin with a brilliant white ground so the colors will appear clear and luminous. To facilitate detail and blending, it must also be smooth and non-absorbent.*

Somehow this description resonates with me. The Thompson's had no idea how their lives were about to contribute so substantially to one girl child's life and her future.

The Priming—Early Childhood

THE DECADE OF the 1940s spawned many changes (upheavals is another appropriate description) in the lives of Canadians. In the first year of that decade the country's population was 11,394,000. Citizens bought a quart of milk for thirteen cents; bread sold for eight cents a loaf and and the average new home required $6,558.OO.

The Liberal party, under the leadership of Honourable W.L. MacKenzie King had been in power since the spring. The government introduced Unemployment Insurance on July 11 of that year.

The carnage of war was deemed inevitable as autumn's blazing colours acquiesced to the blast of winter winds. Internationally, billowing war clouds began to chill the hearts and minds the world over. A touch of reality pierced the haze of denial when Princess Julianna of the Netherlands arrived on June 11 in Ottawa with her two young daughters. She had chosen Canada as a safe country in which to spend her exile as Germany had recently invaded her country. Her husband, Prince Bernard, remained behind to fight on the front lines.

As a magnanimous gesture of gratitude, 200,000 tulip bulbs were delivered to Ottawa shortly after the war was officially declared over. Another 22,000 arrived a year later.

September brought the first installment of prisoners of war (POWs) to Canada. In all, over 30,000 combatants plus several hundred newly arrived "suspicious" individuals were arrested and housed in hastily constructed quarters. Internment camps in various parts of the country were waiting their arrival, including Lethbridge, Medicine Hat and Wainwright, Alberta. Britain, because of the geographical proximity to the Western European battlegrounds,could not accommodate this influx.

The conflict in the domestic venue of Joe and Evelyn had succumbed to a disquieting routine of "life after divorce". Life was good for their wee girl who ended up in a foster home of kind Jehovah Witnesses. These were the years before a highly organized department of Social Services had any input in placements of children deemed "worthy of care". All arrangements were strictly private.

Joe enlisted in the Air Force . Cooking was his forte. His duties allowed him free weekends to visit me. In the summer of 1942 his regiment was called into overseas service. This occurrence could not have been entirely unforeseen, but a sense of panic immediately set in. What was to become of Rosemary Diane?

Apparently he resisted the invitation of his family to become caregivers. Joe harboured a measure of uneasiness about his siblings. Somehow he felt my well-being would be compromised if I was in their care. His intuition proved sadly correct when he returned from the war. I breathe a prayer of thanksgiving when I recall the story. However, the idea of keeping me in the foster home was fraught with anxiety also.

With a heightening sense of apprehension he set out for a church organized camp called "Sunnyside" a few kilometers north Sylvan Lake, Alberta. Perhaps the name "Sunnyside" struck a responsive chord in his spirit due to his childhood upbringing in an area of the same name. His overarching thought was to find a Christian couple who would adopt me. Such a heady ambition, but time was of the essence. A miracle was needed. Immediately.

Marching up the aisle of the 1,300 seat wood frame tabernacle (really a multi-layer of wood shavings), he eased into a bone-aching bench midway up the sanctuary. Persuading the fidgety, golden-haired youngster beside him to sit still was an exercise in futility. How many times had I been in a church service like this? Probably not too many, hence the curiosity and excitement provided by the music and friendly ambiance. I kept turning around and waving "hi" to a middle-aged couple immediately behind. No amount of "sh-h-hing" dissuaded me.

The benediction was pronounced. A wave of courage rose. Turning to Norman and Alice Thompson, married for fifteen years, happy but barren, he mustered the strength to ask the crucial question. No fertility clinics or wondrous pharmaceuticals to urge things along in that era. Both accepted the reality of childlessness with a sense of quiet resignation.

"I can tell my little girl.." he began, "*my little girl really likes you. Would you like to adopt her?*" The words were out. He waited the answer with teary eyes. What a question! The couple to whom it was addressed were totally unknown to him. And, of course, the gentleman was a complete stranger! No background checks. Nothing to verify the truth was being told. In this age of scrutiny and paranoia, an inquiry like that would be certainly unthinkable. A quick call on a cellphone to the nearest R.C.M.P. detachment would probably result.

Reflect for a moment on the shock, the joy, the anticipation! A quick glance between husband and wife--a conversation unspoken- and the forthcoming, unequivocal " YES, YES, YES!". No worries about adjustment on all sides, apparently. My mother's heart informs me unknown arrangements had to be in order. Familiar toys and clothes must have be packed with a sense that this journey was going to end well. Potty training was an assumed "done deed". This was the era previous to disposable diapers and endless patience on the part of parents to await the dawning of "neurological readiness"!

On July 19 it was a *feat accompli*. I drove to Calgary with my new parents, my birth father flew off to serve his country in Europe and my name was changed to Virginia Ruth. An interesting interplay of facts makes my "new" moniker relevant and noteworthy. My birth mother had a cousin named Virginia who died after an accident when she was ten years old. The state of West Virginia would always be held dear to

A Portrait in Progress

Alice with a daughter bearing the appellation.

My earliest recollection is of my public dedication to God in a church on 8th Avenue in Calgary Alberta. In the evangelical church (Pentecostal Assemblies of Canada) where my adoptive parents were members, children were (are!) "dedicated" rather than baptized as infants or "confirmed" as early adolescents.

I walked up to the altar holding the hands of my new Mommy and Daddy. The minister, Rev. George Upton, blessed me with a prayer. Customarily, the parents hand their infant or child to the pastor who then holds him or her up so the congregation can "ooh and ahh' over the sweetie. Well, it didn't happen that way and my child-heart was ..miffed. Fuming at this obvious snub, on the way home I asked why Pastor Upton had not picked me up like he did the others. I can't recall how my parents answered!

I related this story forty years later on a Mother's Day in a branch church that had been "birthed" by that particular assembly. A stately older woman came up to me following the sermon to inform me she was in that service and distinctly recalled the details. Her recounting of the joy exhibited by Alice and Norman moves me to this day.

One incident stands out around the time I was three and a half. A single lady offered to take me for a walk when she went shopping at the local Super Market a few blocks away from our house. She left me at the door of the establishment while she I picked up a few necessities. I became bored. People watching had not yet become a hobby!! I innocently wandered away, crossed a street and became totally befuddled. I knew I had done something wrong by leaving Miss Knowles behind. I ran up and down the street wailing. A Calgary City policeman appeared and took me into another store where he tried to coax me into calmness by the offer of a banana. I remember crying,"*No banana!*" as I squished it between my fingers making a dreadful mess for the officer to try and clean up. When asked my name I replied *"Jeannie Tommy".*

By this time my temporary guardian was in a lather of remorse. Somehow we made our way back to the store where I received a rather chilly welcome. I was scolded for being so imprudent for leaving the location where I had been left in good faith. My mother reiterated the same message. It was a vastly different world in those days! No pampering or sympathy!

Our family moved to Edmonton on the advice of a family doctor. Alice suffered from painful bouts of arthritis which marred previously enjoyed activities. The condition was blamed on the frequent Chinooks which are one of the everlasting features of Calgary. The move proved to be remedial. I do not recall my mom debilitated by painful stiffness thereafter.

Our first home was a rented venue three blocks from the legislative building on 108 Street. One of the daily rituals enjoyed by mother and daughter was watching the red light flicker on at 6 pm every evening. My father was employed as the manager of the Sherwin Williams paint store on Jasper Avenue. Supper was on the table when he arrived home without fail at 5:30 pm each day.

Norman oversaw the construction of a house in the Highlands area of the city. Ada Boulevard was a mere block away with its heritage houses and manicured landscaping. Schools were relatively nearby. One was named Virginia Park. Imagine the coincidence! As with all building dreams that are constructed into reality, hassles of every sort reared their nasty heads. For some reason, the plaster refused to dry causing months of exasperation. A plumber couldn't be found whose middle name was reliability. Shingles were in short supply all over the country. On and on the irritations continued. My father's usual excellent humour faded into black more than once.

In the spring of 1947 we were officially "home". My room was upstairs with a slanted ceiling and a secret space behind one of the closets. New furniture and crisp white bedding were the equivalent of heaven to me. That room with its pale green paint was a hallowed space. The walls saw childish outbursts, teenage angst and the giddiness of true love.

The war ended, peace for all time was declared and Joe Green returned home. He had made arrangements with his brothers a certain amount of money from his armed forces allowance would be banked or invested by them during his tenure in Europe. He planned to buy property upon his return from active duty. It sounded like a good idea. Experience proved otherwise. The money could not be accounted for and no satisfactory reason was forthcoming. His dream vanished. Nursing a heart filled with resentment Joe turned his mind toward northern B.C. to rebuild his shattered life. A very unpleasant welcome for a veteran who had stood in the enemy's path for the sake of his country.

Before moving he visited our home several times. Always introduced as Uncle Joe, I have wonderful memories sitting on his lap, enthralled by his singing. He played a small accordion which seemed to be a magical instrument to my childlike thinking. Recalling those times with my parents in the nineteen eighties, they still referred to him as "Uncle Joe'.

"The priming of a painting must be allowed to dry completely before any more work is carried out". "According to experts the first step involves the application of a shading material which serves as a guide for later utilization of colour and variations in tone. The goal of this step is to keep the rich shading colour as transparent as possible. The dry matte finish will not resist the process of "overpainting" as successive layers of colour are added.

A sense of destiny has always been a part of my thinking. (My eyes are stinging even those words are typed. I am aware how ego-centered they may appear to others). When I was five years old my Sunday School teacher asked me what I was going to do when I grew up. Without a blush or the bat of an eye, I replied " *I am going to be a nurse and work in Africa".* Heady stuff for a pre-kindergarten kid.

A short time before that particular conversation, revival meetings had been held in our church. A radio evangelist by the name of Rev. Sawtell was the invited speaker. An appeal was made at the close of one evening service for people to open their hearts to God and ask Jesus Christ to be their personal savior. I walked up to the altar alone. The evangelist himself knelt beside me and prayed a straight forward, humble request to God to meet this child in such a manner she would be forever aware of His presence. The scripture he used to help me understand the significance of this spiritual encounter was Revelation 3:20. The text he quoted from was the traditional King James Version.

Behold, I stand at the door and knock. If any man hear my voice and open the door, I will come into him and sup with him and he with me.

He explained it was the same as opening the front door after hearing the door bell ring and inviting the person standing there to come on in and have supper with me. No complex theological explanation was necessary. An ancient picture of Christ standing outside a handleless door hung in the foyer of the church. Using this for a pictorial clarification, Rev. Sawtell helped me understand completely.

The rock-bed of spiritual development was initiated. In time, Psalm 139 became my "song" even before I totally comprehended its significance. For example, verses 13-16 from The Message

Oh yes, you shaped me first inside, then out; you formed me in my mother's womb. I thank you, God,--you are breathtaking! Body and soul, I am marvelously made!....You know exactly how I was made, bit by bit, how I was sculpted from nothing into something. Like an open book, you watched me grow from conception to birth; all the stages of my life were spread out before you.

My first experience of school was in a formidable box-like structure called Cromdale School. There were separate entrances for boys and girls. Woe unto the mischievous child who tried to sneak in a door not designated for their gender! One memory was destined to become suspended in time. Miss MacNeil, an elderly teacher/principal strapped a mentally challenged boy for some trifling incident she regarded as insubordination. His little face crumpled and the rest of us sat with unshed tears hoping he wasn't hurting too much. I related the sad scene to my mother, in tears, the narrative being made more poignant because the lad and his parents attended our church.

Another minutiae—my lifelong dependence on eyeglasses began in first grade. The pair was made of gold wire which bent easily and always required cleaning. I was not happy to be the only student whose learning depended on spectacles.

In Grade Two, one day I was disciplined for talking during a reading class. I had to stand outside the door, my misdemeanor obvious to all who walked by. Thoroughly chastened, I was given permission to return to the class after the longest 30 minutes in my life—up to that point! Miss Hall lived a block from us in an austere brick dwelling. From this far off perspective it seemed to match her demeanor. One day I decided she needed salvation. I drew some pictures that resembled flames with the caption if she didn't give her heart to Jesus, she would end up in hell. My dear parents were suitably mortified and my budding career as a hardwired evangelist was cut off at the knees!

A growing awareness gripped me during those early years of elementary school. I inwardly felt I was somewhat "different" than my cousins and the other kids at school. A visiting relative looked at me one day and murmured, *"Is she the little one Alice and Norman got?"* WHAT DID THAT MEAN?

I had no siblings, my parents were older than my friends', no resemblance to ANYBODY close at hand. Putting all these clues together I decided that I came from somewhere else, although the love of the Thompsons was never in doubt. I must have been adopted—someone gave me up. This never became an unbearable burden or an insufferable obsession. I just had to know for sure. My intuitive self was kicking in. Pestering my parents brought no satisfaction. Their repeated answer to every inquiry, no matter how coyly it was framed, was always the same, *"You belong to us and we love you".* The reply seemed a bit hollow to a third grader.

Miss Watson occupied the teacher's chair the year my curiosity outflanked my patience. Her thin, sharply delineated features were congruent with her teaching methods. She made it a point to stride up and down between the rows of desks, looking (perhaps, hunting is the preferred term here) for dwarf-sized smudges, arithmetic mistakes or spelling errors. Such entities were never hard to find. A whack on the head (boys) or a smack on the knuckles (girls) was the reward for such slovenliness. Perhaps on this particular day I was on the receiving end of her hard-edged ruler. My memory is porous at this point. Whatever happened close to the final bell unleashed a torrent of rage. I ran the three blocks to the house, clamored up to my room and proceeded to have a full-blown tantrum. Kicking and screaming, I yelled at mother, *"If you don't tell me whether or not I am adopted, I'm gonna run away!"*

Poor Alice. She was more frightened of me disappearing in a fit of pique than disclosing the truth. Tears streaming down her face, she gently confessed that yes, indeed, I was adopted. The scene ended abruptly. I told myself I had been right all along. What was the big deal anyhow? The issue was never raised again. I wore the fact I was "chosen" like an invisible badge of merit.

Raised as a solitary singleton adoptee meant my view of family life was ...rather narrow. Sibling rivalry was a definite unknown entity. It took marriage to begin the process of understanding the principles of sharing, compromise and negotiation, although having a roommate in nurses' training was an enormous kick-start!

My grade 4 teacher was a tall handsome man who managed to create plenty of rumours about his activities. He taught his homeroom class art twice a week. During one of those sessions we were instructed to incorporate our initials into a drawing. He then made a point of evaluating on the spot. He glanced at mine and said, looking over his reading glasses, *"That's not very creative, Virginia".*

To say I was crushed is the least mild way I felt. Of course it was a childish rendering! This statement stuck with me for decades. Its untruth wove a veil across my heart in such a way I grew to believe I was hopeless in any endeavour which required an artistic touch.

The word "cancer" with all its connotations sprang into my

consciousness in Grade 5. Miss Morrow, with the lovely hair had married over the summer holidays, and now had become Mrs. Gowan to everyone, missed many weeks of classes. Finally near to Christmas of that year, the principal let it be known Mrs. Gowan had passed away.

Junior High School meant a brisk walk to Highlands school, about a mile away. Mrs. Savage, Mr. Gish, Mrs Lago—all played a part in who I became. In literature class we were spellbound by Dicken's *"Tale of Two Cities"*. An added incentive to understand the novel was the movie that summed up the story perfectly. I felt a sense of disgust at Madame LaFarge--*"How could she keep knitting while all those heads rolled into the basket?"* However, because movies were viewed as nasty tools of Satan, the fact I was not struck dead or immobilized with palsy, seemed to be nothing short of miraculous.

Eastglen Composite High School was a mere four blocks from our home on 70th Street. Choosing the matriculation stream of courses engendered no angst because of the firm conviction I was destined to become a registered nurse had never lessened. In grade 10 I had a searing crush on a senior student named Emanuel Evans. This good-looking young man owned a black Volkswagen "Beetle" embellished with sparkling decals pasted in important places. One day he asked me to meet him outside following the last class. Naturally I assumed I would not be walking home that chilly day. Well. BIG surprise! Dear Emanuel only wanted to check out the time of an upcoming youth crusade. After getting that information, he hopped into his car and off he drove! I stomped home muttering "CAD" under my breath and cried as the ardor abruptly faded.

Scanning the regularly maintained diary entries reveal a streak of sassiness long forgotten. Two examples which show this:

March 31, 1955—Mr Naciuk is SO UNFAIR. I should've had 12 more marks on my health test. I told him so after school and he gave the marks back to me. Yea!!

September 28 (Wednesday)--Today I told Mr. Brown I did not believe half of the stuff he told us. He sure was embarrassed.

At what point did I lose this ability to stand up to authority figures? When did the courage to address perceived injustice evaporate?

In 1956 the A and W fast food establishment blew into our city and suddenly THAT was the place to be and to be seen. Any old "cad" could become a respectable date if he included a jaunt to the nearest Mama and Papa drive-in. In the spring of that year an opportunity to teach Sunday School presented itself. The venue was Montrose Elementary School. Apparently my parents figured I was stable enough spiritually to miss Sunday morning worship services. Teaching grade three kids that year was an initiation into a life long avocation. Hours were spent every week cutting out flannel graph pictorials. In addition each child had something to take home after the teaching time.

One of the other teachers was Bob Cornish. A young teenager, ready to smack the whole world in its face, became unruly and disrespectful during one of the sessions. It seemed he was genetically wired to annoy anyone who came into his space. After enduring his jittery antics for a while, Bob asked him kindly to leave the room. He flounced out , shouting one memorable line, *"You are a big SHOT spelled with an I !!"* A rendering today of that parting farewell would not be so sanitary!

The shadow of my cousin Norma (six months my senior with the same middle name) cast itself frequently on my pathway. She was beautiful, blond and had the important measurements I longed for. Her dating schedule seemed chockablock full compared to mine. Two young men even had a duel (in the church basement, would you believe!) over who loved her the most. Did I ever have such an expression of ardor? Nah. Lots of Friday evenings after Young Peoples I'd catch an Edmonton transit bus home, knowing full well Norma was with Bob, Maver or Dave.

A well-dressed young woman in that era coveted "slim jims" more than any other fashion statement. Her closet housed at least one tartan skirt and several straight tweeds, if she was lucky. Bobby socks coupled with white buck shoes or camel-hued sahara boots made the difference between "sharp" and "ho hum".

A merchant friend of my father (who at the time was manager of the Sherwin Williams paint store on Jasper Ave) had an upscale women's ready-to-wear shop. Charlie Rapp gave me a part-time clerking position with after school hours. Surrounded by the latest fashions, I was deliciously happy. The slow times were passed by musing how I could coordinate my wardrobe if I ever earned enough money to buy the outfits displayed. The hourly wage was a grand seventy-five cents!

I drooled over a yellow angora sweater and imagined myself wearing it to an evening party with black shiny shoes. I hadn't been "colour draped" at that age so had no idea yellow was definitely NOT my colour. The epitome of my fashion purchases was a demure silk half-slip in ravishing fuschia. Cuddled in tissue paper, it found its place in my hope chest. It became a part of my honeymoon regalia seven years later!

Typing was an easy credit. The day I finally managed to type sixteen (16!) words a minute was special. I duly noted it in my diary pages.

Several notations about my acne punctuate the pages which otherwise seem rather carefree. Case in point is the April 24 entry--

> Boy!! I am desperate about my skin. The order of the day is no sweets. I have to find the willpower, but I am finally getting some. Got a purse--$4.98. That's very expensive, but I can't help it.

A couple of months earlier I had written the following, obviously in a more playful mood.

> I had loads of work so I didn't go to church. Norma's party was a riot! I can hold 7 big marshmallows in my mouth. We played Telegram, Rhythm and Fruit Basket. Someone stepped on my foot—and BINGO, a hole in my stocking

It was required to wear prescribed gym uniforms for all Phys. Ed classes. A kind description follows—ugly pea green rompers with puffy sleeves and buttoned up tops.

All students in grade 12 were required to write exams called departmentals in all core subjects. My hopes and dreams were fastened to these exams. During the month of August waiting for the results was a test of endurance. I was a camp counselor to elementary school girls for several weeks to help alleviate the anxiety. The letter was finally hand delivered by my dad who drove down to our cabin on Sylvan Lake to deliver the document.

Out went quiet Canadian deportment! Norma, who incidentally was in similar circumstances, joined me as we hooted and hollered *"We made it! We are going to be nurses!"* racing back to our respective cottages. Our young females charges were forgotten as we tasted the ecstasy of the moment.

Scattered throughout the pages, describing passionate details of my worldview, are numerous references to the trips my parents and I took frequently. Sand was sprinkled (so to speak!) in my shoes by grade 6. We traveled across Canada three times, by rail and car. Scandinavian relatives welcomed us in Wisconsin, Minnesota and the Dakotas. The lure of far-off places has never faded.

Early Flemish painters planned the initial stages of their work with great care. Those tedious first steps became the backbone of their finished work of art. Important details and contours were included. They facilitate the necessary skill to layer the oil paints at a later date. A process called "underpainting" was designed to combine with the later stages to produce the desired effect.

As I reflect on my formative years I clearly see a few parallels. The thrust into a teaching mode, albeit without serious training and only on weekends, became a way of life for me later on. Learning to adapt and appreciate a variety of geography as well as sleeping accommodations would serve me well in the succeeding years.

Nursing/Midwifery/Theological College

WHEN I ENTERED the halls of the University of Alberta Hospital in the autumn of 1958, my view of family life took a profound shaking. The stories I heard from my classmates and patients confirmed my parents marriage was not the norm. Alice and Norman Thompson had a "liberated marriage" long before the phrase was formulated. By that I mean they shared the load of gardening, housework and so on—never acting as though a particular job was classified by gender riggings that made it unacceptable to the other. They were a TEAM and my world was the winner!

Norma and I were roommates the first year. The experience of sharing a tiny room was excellent discipline for me. The rules that governed the nurses' residence seem quaint and frankly bizarre from this vista. Our room was inspected every month by appointed senior students. I imagine they got a hefty supply of titters as they marched from room to room noting grievous lapses of tidiness/cleanliness. Unhappily, it was my side of the living space that always earned warning notes--"*This side is very messy. Please have it in order when I come around in 24 hours!*"

We were assigned a seat in the lecture hall during the very first class. It was ours for the next three years. The young woman next to

Nursing/Midwifery/Theological College

me was named Ursula. It seemed as she was always under the weather as she lurched from crisis to crisis. For some demented reason I kept a note she furtively wrote me during a microbiology class given by a professor we dubbed Dr. Fungihead.

I just hate this crap! I wish I could SCREAM!!!!

His monotone presentations lulled us into a state akin to comatose. The reality that the information he was trying his hardest to make us swallow, was unpronounceable as well as frightening in prospect, made no difference to our weary brains. Protozoa, viruses, rickettsiae, fungi, mycoplasma pneumonia, obligate anaerobe---we had to know them all.

Ursula loved to decant a perfume called *"Emeraude".* Recalling the stench of it at this moment is raising hives between my toes. At our thirty fifth reunion in central B.C. I could tell it was still her favorite scent. At one point she grabbed my arm during a pause in the activities and poured out a litany of ills. To emphasize her state of poor health she displayed a picture of herself, lying on a fancy rug, naked except for panties and a top covering of her bust. Yes, she was unusually skinny but really now....the visual impact was a bit too much. The shock value was sufficient to produce gagging. By a providential act of grace I restrained myself and saved the dramatics for later! Her divorce from a prominent entrepreneur only granted her three million dollars plus an elegant cabin on Lake Invermere. " *Lord have mercy,* I thought, *I would be glad to have the tithe of that!"* I wish her peace. She passed away years ago.

I remember being horrified at the sassiness and rude remarks which Dr. Metcalfe peppered throughout his lectures on urology. I was ushered into the "real world" where language was neither edited or sanitized. So different than around my home. The evening I inquired what the word now known as the "F-bomb" meant, the look on my mother's face told me I had crossed the line of expected deportment. For all I knew it could have been Yiddish for rutabaga! Just inquiring caused Alice to appear as though she was in the midst of a cardiac event.

Our "probie" uniforms were a faded blue striped, with a pinafore of stiffly starched white cotton. A modest hemline was enforced by measuring the number of inches from ground level. Sensible black oxfords with matching hose completed the look. Our allowance was twelve dollars monthly which began after a six month probation period. A capping ceremony (now relegated to the corridors of remembrance) was a highlight that initial year. Marching into a hall filled with proud parents and siblings wishing us the best served to remind us to carry on inspite of fatigue and the fear of not being capable of holding up the high standard Florence Nightingale had set for herself during troubled times in the Crimean War. We were presented with white Gideon Bibles, small replica lamps and the standard white caps which designated us as UAH nurses. Ceremonies such as this are symbolic of something higher than ourselves. 'Tis a pity they have vanished.

The first article I wrote for publication was for "*The Torch*", official organ of the Gideons, an organization committed to the free distribution of the Bible. The editor asked for my personal feeling about the significance of the presentation. My father was a longtime member of this business men's group. It was a thrill to see my name in print!

An enormous amount of bafflegab surrounds the state of affairs in our provincial health care system. This has centered mainly on the cost as well as management systems. Gasping and croaking always occurs around the topic of rising costs. True enough. One subject I have never heard addressed is the fact student nurses and medical interns were given responsibility far beyond what is now considered appropriate and were rewarded with very little remuneration. The thought of a first year nursing student in charge of a thirty bed surgical ward on an evening shift is now incomprehensible! As the medical world and its devotees progressed, so did compensation. Of course costs have risen due to other factors, but it is noteworthy to acknowledge the effort of students who managed to keep the gears running smoothly without complaining.

Nursing/Midwifery/Theological College

In second year (uniforms were now a tepid pink hue) I was elected president of the Student Nurses Association. This position gave me the opportunity to address various interested groups (new students included) . I discovered stage fright was not part of the package for me personally. It was fun to present new ideas to interested people. The best part was a free trip to Banff to represent my hospital at the annual convention of the Alberta Association of Registered Nurses. It involved traveling by train. As the train chugged into Edmonton's Southside station one of the other delegate's suitcase seized that moment to split open. Panic mixed with hilarity describes the scene perfectly. An employee at the station managed to find a length of rope which was hastily bound around the gaping valise. We were billeted in the old King Edward hotel in Banff. The only intrusion into our happiness was the brown-tinged water that poured from the taps. Apologies were proffered by the management but not one of us ventured to take a bath.

I learned through experience sometimes the opinion of the majority is not necessarily divine truth. Most of my classmates adored the nurse in charge of Station 54-Neurology, Miss Pamela Watts. It seemed as though a mutual admiration society had blossomed in the byways of the hospital. Everyone left her floor with glowing ward reports. Not so with this student. Her apparent dislike for me increased with every shift. As a result, I failed my final report from her. She called me into her austere office and grimly told me my fate, She told me if I ever graduated she truly hoped I would not choose to work on a neurological unit. It was a humiliating lesson.

On the other hand I listened to alarming reports about the clinical instructor on pediatrics. My feet were leaden as I trudged up to the children's ward for my first day of duty. Surprise. *Lovely* surprise. Mrs. Mackintosh and I managed famously together in a genuine learning atmosphere. Several years later I was her nurse in the delivery room. She took my hand between contractions and told me I was one of the best students she had ever taught! Hm-m-mm. One speaks strange things when under duress.

The beginning of our third year of instruction meant we exchanged the hideous black work shoes and stockings for white footwear and hose. You had to be there to taste the exhilaration of this achievement. The traditional romp down to the high level bridge with shoes and tattered stockings was newsworthy every year. Once lined up along the railing we raised the conglomeration representing our first two years of training. With a glorious shout followed by a mighty thrust, dozens of shoes were swept to a watery grave in the North Saskatchewan River. Can't imagine the eco-minded folks of today smiling about that.

One of the young male patients I nursed on the polio unit in 1959 won "The Most Outstanding University Professor" award in all of Canada in 1997. I heard him interviewed by Michael Enright on C.B.C. shortly thereafter.

Life at any stage involves change. During our senior year the entire student body was informed the design of our most venerable nurse's cap was about to be altered. Complaints from former grads working in various parts of Canada indicated the design was difficult to launder and iron. Such distress descended especially to the class of September '61...my class. We were to be the first ones to graduate wearing the newly designed cap. WELL-L-L, that proclamation triggered a revolt!! We certainly WERE NOT -read our collective lips- going to desecrate our heads with a silly new cap. We would go on strike before we would capitulate to anyone telling us what to do. My, my....the energy expended on what proved to be a fruitless endeavour.

Our director of nursing, Miss Jeannie Clarke, began to wear various samples of caps that were under scrutiny by the faculty in order to make an "appropriate" choice. We muffled the snorts of derision every time she walked into the cafeteria with a new sample on her perfectly coiffed head. But then, a shift occurred. We were indeed the first class to be issued the new cap. Our pride on being the initial graduates to don the cap went beyond belief.

Within the quick daily notations in my diaries from '58 to '61 are revealing items of joy as well sorrow, frustration and just a touch of disillusionment.

Nursing/Midwifery/Theological College

> *October 31, 1958: Wonderful service this evening. Believe I got my call to be a missionary confirmed. George Labercane did some great skits. Asked Maureen to come, but she couldn't.*
>
> *October 23, 1959: Mrs. McGugan had her hernia operation. She insisted on going to the B.R. despite her catheter. Her IV went interstitial. Just great! We went anyway. But then she got up on her own and in walked her son, Dr.McGugan. He asked me WHY she was allowed up, and I tried to explain. He then told the evening supervisor about me. I feel sick. Next I spilled some soup on my uniform, slipped on some water. Dr.McGugan asked another student to sit with his mother for the rest of the shift. (not a word about me, tho').I talked to Dr. Low afterwards and felt better.*
>
> *July 10, 1960: I feel discouraged. Thought I saw Al in the crowd, but obviously I didn't. I wish I could make up my mind. I should have never come in training.*

(The gentleman mentioned in the above entry was my first true love. It was a difficult decision to say no to a commitment that seemed promising, but my eyes were set on an overseas mission).

Around this time I was invited to an Edmonton Eskimo football game. Johnny Bright and Normie Qwong were the big heroes of the day. It was liberating to feel excited about an activity that didn't involve prayer, memorization, rule keeping or pharmaceutical side effects.

I am reminded by scanning the entries I had more dating relationships than previously remembered! A thread of Providence can be traced which protected me from giving my heart away in a marriage situation. Wilhart—his obesity in later years made him old before his time. Switzer—an abuse issue subsequently destroyed his family. Andre Garden—a fourth year medical student whose communication skills were slightly lower than a front end loader. (I am trying to be polite). I now realize I was in love with the concept of being the spouse of a doctor. On one date the ENTIRE evening was spent explaining the intricate veinous and tendon structure of my left hand. Did he not notice my ring finger looked terribly bare?

"*Who cares?*" I thought as the evening wore down. Perhaps he was rehearsing for an oral exam or something. It was a journey of self-discovery. All the seductive brilliance of a future with a famous (hopefully!) surgeon paled when what I really longed for was a chance to share his heart as well as his home. Dr. Garden stood me up on my 21st birthday. The handwriting was on the wall and it needed no translation. In amongst my papers was a copy of the letter I wrote him.

Dear Andrew,

I trust you had a happy Christmas. Thank you for the card. This is a rather hard letter to write because I'm not sure everything will come out the way I want it to. I want you to send my picture back ASAP. After dating for 2 years, it is quite obvious you are no longer interested in me—not that you ever were. Looking over the past 2 years, I can see some glaring errors I made. One of them was having faith in you. I guess you just never had enough nerve to tell me you had plans for your life which didn't include me. I began to see the light last year and I suppose this letter should have been written then instead of now.

Anyway, this will save you the trouble of preparing a letter or a speech of your own. I will chalk this affair up to experience and look forward to the coming year a little more wise.

Wishing you the best in your career as a doctor and hoping you never have to swallow your own medicine. It's bitter, believe me. Sincerely,

Loss recovery was swift and without incident. A month later a mutual acquaintance informed me he was telling his friends he could get me back any time he wanted. *"Over my dead cadaver"* was the most suitable reply I could think of!

As 1961 rolled in with general jubilation, my plans for the future began to take form. On the night of my graduation I was presented with the "Bedside Nursing Award". The prize was a $35 check along with a letter stating my classmates had honoured me with the achievement.

Obstetrics was tugging my heart toward post-graduate studies in midwifery. Working full time ($285 per month) allowed me to build up a bank account which covered my university tuition. The University of Alberta at that time had a course entitled "Advanced Practical Obstetrics". The closely knit class, composed of young women across Canada and the U.S., was tutored by a passionate teacher, Ms. Margaret Madden.

My practicum was served in Drumheller's Municipal Hospital, deep in Alberta's dinosaur country. I was housed in the nurses' residence so I could be "on call" 24/7. Under the supervision of Dr. Roy LeRiche, I delivered my required quota of 20 babies. The most memorable delivery was that of a Hutterite woman who had previously given birth to seven sons. We all fervently prayed this baby would be a girl. Alas, a male baby burst into the world coughing and cooing as though he knew our supplications should have begun nine months previous! The delighted smile on that mother's face told us it didn't matter.

Attaching myself to a lively local church assembly, I had my first taste of pastoral ministry. Rev. E.C. O'Brien and his dynamo wife Ida, invited me to become involved in the church activities. It was a hectic few months before returning to finish the requisite course of studies.

For some time I had felt my wings sprouting, that is, the need to fly somewhere "exotic" to extend my education into the realm of theology. An application was signed and forwarded to Central Bible College (now Evangel College) in Springfield, Missouri in the early months of 1962. As a Canadian I needed a visa which would allow me to work part time. Money doesn't cascade from the heavens on golden ribbons tied to angels wings. Unfortunate reality.

One horrid week two incidents posing as serious setbacks to the future, offered me the opportunity to really get serious about faith and trust plus a lot of other good things I had been taught. The young woman who only months previous had been accepted into the same program phoned to inform me she had changed her mind. College was not in her future. I found out later a new beau had appeared who evidently was more fun than exams. We had planned on rooming together. BOO! A few days later a crisp note from the American Immigration Bureau told me I was ineligible for a student visa. The reason was high on my "baloney meter". DOUBLE BOO! My well-planned life was falling apart and I'd only begun to live. So I thought. In order to sort out the dilemma by myself and hold in the disappointment, I told no one.

During the final week of post-graduate studies I was assigned to the Outpatient Department of the University Hospital. It was a privilege to help these post-partum moms as they faced critical times. Just before a lunch break the instructor pulled me aside into a curtained cubicle. She startled me by saying in a stage whisper,"*I have no idea what the problem is, but God told me to let you know He will be with you and everything is going to be alright!*" Suddenly the waiting area became a cathedral. A phenomenal sense of peace overtook me. I walked out of that small place , humbled by the hallowing of the Spirit's presence. It proved to be the initial lesson in letting go and letting the Divine accomplish what was best. Those quiet, prophetic words were just what I needed to hear, even though I had proactively planned the coming months.

Peace and reluctance *can* co-exist if one has the patience to keep walking without trepidation about the unknown. I sent in an application to a local college, Canadian Northwest Bible College. Enclosed in the envelope was a tiny bit of aggravation. No problem admitting that. Within days an acceptance letter was in my hand. Financially this was a sensible plan, but the Edmonton setting lacked the cosmopolitan ambiance for which I longed. I expected to gain basic theological training there. Perhaps in a few years I could head out to another fine institution—out of the country, somewhere, anywhere except my home province.

On the first day of classes in September of '62, the registrar invited me to assist her handing out textbooks. My task was to check the names, required fees and insure the allocation of text books as the day progressed. One young man, recently arrived from Kenya where his parents were career missionaries, took his turn in the lineup. I asked him his name, and he replied, *"Jess Lynn"*. I mistakenly thought he said *"Jeslyn"*, so I brightly asked for his last name.

"Lynn is the last name", he said with a bit of an attitude.

"Okay, okay, so I misunderstood. Such a humourless lad" I told myself grimly.

It wasn't many weeks into the semester when it became quite apparent that young man had taken a definite shine to me. The rules which governed dating relationships were strict and compliance was expected. Each Friday there was a long lineup in front of the principal or his deputy's office. Students were waiting for a social permit, an official piece of paper, which allowed them to be in the company of a member of the opposite sex ONE time during the weekend. The permit had to be carried at all times during the date, and produced on demand if a faculty member required it. True love actually blossomed in such a Draconian atmosphere.

I was in immediate demand for the job of accompanying trios, the college choir, a male quartet and various ensembles. My schedule rapidly became bloated with vocal and organ lessons also. As if the rigors of all this plus classes and the incumbent assignments was not enough, I also worked part time (night shift) at the General Hospital. I became very clever at sleeping with my eyes wide open as often I would finish a shift at 7 a.m., grab a small breakfast and be in class at 8 a.m.

I kept a note I wrote Jess during one of those stressful times. (Is the habit of pack-ratting a genetic characteristic??!) It is undated, but Christology was a first year subject so it must have been the winter of '62 or the spring of the following year.

> *12:30 a.m. Hi Honey! I am sitting here in semidarkness and for one plugged nickel I wish I was at home. I gathered you weren't feeling too gay when I left. Please don't be upset— the LORD knows our needs and has promised to meet them. I needed this job---really I did. It bothers me that it had to derive*

us of our devotions together. I trust you understand my position re:next Saturday and the wedding. I'm not anxious about going, but I don't want Sherry to feel I'm not interested. I have just finished marking your Christology notes. I'm sure I shall have a good night, that is I'll have a bit of time for studying and so on. Love as always, Virginia

Working nights at a Roman Catholic hospital was my initial foray into a religious world unlike my own. Every morning the pre-op patients were prepared for communion along with the prescribed sedation. Woe unto the nurse who failed to set the patients up properly for communion!

Jess was two and a half years younger than me which at first precluded his eligibility, or so I originally mused. After our first date (I drove as he had no car at the time), my mother took me aside and solemnly declared that Jess wanted to marry me. Stifling my laughter, I told her she was WAY OFF THE MARK. After three dates I was no longer laughing and she was planning the wedding!

My father sat on the board of governors of the college during my stint there. One morning the president called me into his office and admonished me the expectations were higher for me than the other students because of my father's position. I maintained a cloak of calmness in his presence, but exploded later at a coffee break—all with due decorum expected of a theological student, you must understand.

In between all the frantic activities of college life, Jess and I found the time and energy to plan a future together. Our gift mix seemed to be balanced and harmonious. Being youthful spirits, we were ready for anything the ministry could toss our way.

One of my extracurricular activities included responsibilities with *The Fountain,* the college year book. I had responsibilities from editing to article assignments. The work involved hours and sweat equity which left me personally drained. A request to be the editor in my final year of studies was a burden I declined. When I read an entry dated November 7, 1963, I understood my reasoning perfectly.

> *Man, what a day. First to classes, then to the dentist at 1 p.m. He just "painted" my front teeth. Then home for lunch. Rushed back for an organ lesson at MacDougal United church. Drove down to church for choir practice, then back to Alberta College for a vocal lesson. Grabbed a sandwich in the Waffle Shop before going back for another rehearsal. I AM DEAD TIRED.*

Most of the weekends were spent in student ministry in various churches throughout the province. Once your name was posted on the assignment, you were expected to be in your place Sunday morning, come hell or high water or in some cases, foul weather. One memorable Saturday afternoon the male quartet (Jess was the tenor and I was the pianist-- cosy!) was on its way to Lethbridge when a sudden squall closed Highway 2. A vehicle back ended us as we sat waiting for the traffic to move. It was a shaken group of students that made arrangements for another car. Around the supper hour we were on our way again, but not without doubts concerning the wisdom of the trip. We had been told it was compulsory.

Another weekend a late spring storm, blinding in its fury, did little to deter a busload of eager students homebound from Calgary. Even then I pondered the concept of putting ministry before safety. Miraculously, no one was ever injured or cars irretrievably damaged.

First year ended on a couple of high notes. I was selected as the representative of my class to speak at the commencement ceremony in 1963. The next weekend Jess and I were invited to spend the weekend with friends in the Drumheller area. (School was out for the summer so we didn't have to ask for one of those pesky "social permits")

The diary entry of April 19 explains it all.

> *I AM IN LOVE. I AM IN LOVE. I found out for sure on the top of the Nacmine Outlook. We climbed the HooDoos earlier in the day. Great fun. Wind and Dust+++*

A Portrait in Progress

The months and assignments rolled along. Jess and I were certain we would spend the rest of our lives together, madly in love and passionate about the ministry. We chose my engagement ring during a jewelry sale at Klein's Jewelers on Jasper Avenue. The lovely solitaire was a grand $200-- a huge price for a poor college student to sacrifice. The rules stated that permission had to be obtained before a couple became engaged. A little rebellion now and then is a good thing! A few weeks after that precious ring was tucked away, my beloved made an appointment with the principal to secure the required dispensation.

The evening before Jess left for a summer stint in Hay River he placed it on my finger and I flew into ecstasy. My parents, however, were not quite so elated. They loved Jess, but he had neglected to ask my hand in marriage from them. A big OOPS. They quickly recovered and the incident was never mentioned again.

I had secured a 3 month position as an R.N. in a mission health care setting, the H.H. Williams Memorial Hospital in Hay River, Northwest Territories. The pay was $90 per month—room and board included. Staff was hard to procure so 12 hour shifts and long stretches of 14 days at a time were rather common. I have a cache of unbelievable experiences that cause eye-rolling when I hear of the "hardships" encountered in contemporary medical facilities today.

Its true. The North does get in your blood once you have tasted the extended summer days with the heightened sense of community that springs from living with folks from divergent backgrounds. Listening to interesting narratives from a global perspective was soul-enhancing.

During the last portion of my tenure I developed a raging abscess on a front tooth. No one was available to relieve me on a frantic night shift. The shot of penicillin I had been given was a year and a half past its due date. Naturally, it was not effective! I soldiered on praying the night would take of itself. In walked an R.C.M.P. Constable (always a sign of something bad happening which needed a doctor). He took a dismissive look at me and said, *"Where's Virginia? I need her."* I looked at him and said, *"Bob, its me!"*

"Holy Moses! What happened to you?" he blurted out.

Jess was a born handyman-fixer. His summer job at the same mission hospital was "official go-fer". A wide range of duties were assigned to him which I suppose was a pre-missionary training stint.

One afternoon, with a couple of hours to spare before an evening shift, we took a lazy spin in a rickety boat down the Hay River. It was fun, romantic even, until the sheer pin fractured. We were in the middle of nowhere with a moribund motor. Suddenly the pressing dilemma twisted romantic into frantic. No cell phones to pry help from somewhere. With limited tools, excellent skills and substantial prayer, the motor belched into service and off we took. I was late for my duties and no one of course believed the sheer-pin story!!!

Grocery bills were atrocious, then as now once the 60th parallel is traversed. I ached for a bar of Philadelphia crème cheese. One week the local grocer had it on hand. Once it was in my hands I couldn't wait to get it in my mouth. Opening the package resulted in gagging and outright disgust. I had paid heavy money for this item which was blue from mold, top to bottom!

My father promised Alice he would take her to Ireland the year he retired. He agreed to include me in this special sojourn if I could get permission to miss the opening weeks of college in the autumn of 1964. It was an emotional homecoming for him as he had not returned since emigrating in 1919.

Senior year was upon us, and each member of *"The Conquerors"* began to gear up for future ministry now that graduation was in view. In my stack of memorabilia is a note from my closest friend at college, herself newly married to a classmate. I do not recall the incident, but her note elucidates the feeling.

Dear Jess: Sorry for trying on Virginia's ring. I didn't know it bothered or affected you. If I had known I wouldn't have done it. So sorry again and my humble apology. So please cheer up and don't look upset or you'll upset Virginia too, OK?

Laughable from this viewpoint!

A Portrait in Progress

On graduation night in April of 1965 I was thrilled to be the valedictorian of *The Conquerors '65*. Three weeks later I was a blushing bride walking down the aisle of Central Tabernacle in Edmonton to begin another era as a "newbie" clergywife.

We had known for six weeks a small congregation in Vulcan, Alberta would be ours to shepherd. A tragedy had taken the life of the pastor's wife a day after she had given birth to a baby son. Leaving the ministry was the only option he could see in the devastating circumstance. Unaccustomed to the grief process ourselves, we walked into the midst of group of people who were not really ready for us. Nor we for them.

Jess and I arrived at our designated abode after a honeymoon in Central Canada. A word of wisdom, just in case anyone is attentive at this juncture. Honeymooning with in-laws is not in my book of recommendations for a happy life. Too much to absorb. Too little kitchen experience. Enough said. The best part of all was getting to know Janice and Jillian, Jess's sisters.

We lived in the basement of the church which meant the bathroom facilities were shared with the congregation. The kitchen and living room was used on Sundays to accommodate Christian Education classes. What that meant in practical terms was a 30 minute portion from Hades each Sabbath morn as I raced around trying to make our home look "decent and spiritual" before I took my place at the piano.

Somehow a hallowed aura surrounds those years, but nostalgia is noticeably absent! Because the kitchen was directly beneath the sanctuary, the timing of the benediction coincided nicely with the aroma of dinner (cooking itself to perfection in the oven) as it wafted up through the air vents. Hand designed cotton curtains, Blue Mountain pottery, 18 china tea cups and saucers, the brown striped hide-a-bed we purchased with wedding gift money---the memories press me now.

One day a dehydrated mouse dropped out of a macaroni package. God only knows how long it had been there. The Ladies group gave us a food shower every once in a while. One time they *carefully* cut off the labels from some canned vegetables and glued them on

Nursing/Midwifery/Theological College

to different containers. Naturally I was puzzled when I opened a can which told me green peas lay within, and out dropped orange carrots! As a diligent consumer, I was concerned that someone else, less equipped to handle a cardiac event, would perhaps view this onerous episode as a reason to sue. I contacted *Libby's and Company* and gently exhorted them on Quality Assurance. I only found out about the ruse after I told the ladies about the matter. They laughed until they cried. And the dear company in question sent me back six cans with correct labels!

One Sunday in November of that first year in Vulcan we had a visit from a cousin of Jess's who was on the first lap of a 'round the world trip. Kenneth Lynn had just finished a stint with the R.C.M.P. In Prince Edward Island. He eventually fulfilled his dream of traveling the world and ended up with a number of unbelievable stories of impossible adventures. On our bulletin board in the downstairs family room is a snapshot of myself between Jess and Kenneth. Courage would have failed me if on that day I could have spied the future. 'Tis a blessing the future is veiled. What intrigue that picture held! It was a precursor of things to come.

Our firstborn son, Regan Thompson, made his appearance on a Sunday. Sunday is the absolute worst day for a child of the manse to be born (my opinion for which I accept responsibility). We drove into Calgary in a pre-dawn dash. My young husband dropped me at the General Hospital's labour and delivery ward, and then drove home to conduct the morning worship service. How attentive was the congregation that morning? What was the sermon's text? I laboured alone all day. Phoned him shortly after the evening service ended to inform him he was a father. Who was there to congratulate him? Who was there to share my joy?

Dr. Higgins, my ob-gyn doctor, had just returned from a tropical vacation. During my hours of labour I told the nurses I had a breech baby. They informed me I was mistaken. Only when a cute little butt made its presence known did they panic and agree with me. Regan was hustled off to the Neo-Natal Intensive Care Nursery. For 24 hours I did not see him, and NO explanation was forthcoming. On Tuesday morning I marched down to the nursery and asked to speak to the supervisor. She was unaware I had not been informed about the diagnosis of cerebral edema as a result of the breech delivery. Her apologies seemed so trite considering the anxiety we had endured. Thank goodness for prayer chains and the good people who are committed to that ministry. All was well in the end and a happy trio returned home the following week.

I harboured resentment for years because of what I considered "ministry before maternity". Jess and I were only able to talk about my feelings when he was in the terminal stage of his life. He apologized with tears for that lapse of judgment.

Regardless of our glaring ignorance about *real* life, we were loved by that congregation. Valuable lessons about governing, figuring out border personalities and budgeting were gleaned from our two and a half years spent there. Not once were we stung by criticism of our clothes, visitation routines, boring sermons or anything else which fuels discontent. Every special season -harvest, Christmas, Easter- the congregation brought food baking goods, garden produce, and meat to decorate the front of the altar. Do congregations do that anymore? The gestures were a wonderful way to supplement our meager wage.

One older couple were the primary charter members. I grew weary of listening to them as they expounded the exploits of the founding pastor's wife. It was as though they had purchased a majority of shares in a company named *"Original Adoration Society"*! She was an energetic mother who managed her family (5 kids!). the church and the whole town. Seemed like that anyway. My inexperience seemed dim-witted when compared to this glorious former clergywife. A number of years later, during a provincial church conference, I felt supremely vindicated when a succeeding pastor's wife told me she was tired of hearing all the good things about ME! It made my day. Maybe even my month!

Working part-time at the local nursing home gave me a small salary which eased the frequent monetary crunch. As I read the May 21,1967 entry, a familiar shiver of angst swept over me.

Surprise! 37 in S.S. For the third Sunday in a row. Tollefsons down to visit. The congregation gave us $13 for an anniversary gift. Actually had a p.m. Service. Regan was good in both services. The car needs a motor job, so says Dennis, to the tune of $150. Oh Lord, help us now, please!

Jess was ordained in the summer of '67 thereby opening the door for appointment as an overseas missionary candidate. In September we received a missive that explained we met the requirements for overseas mission work. We were bound for Liberia, West Africa. That information came to us when we were vacationing in Ontario. We drove back planning to break the news to our beloved congregation the following Sunday. To our dismay, word of our appointment had preceded us. Our people already knew and were beginning the process of detachment.

When we informed my parents of this exciting development, my mother started to cry. Through tears of agony she managed weakly to say," *But that is the land of the white man's grave".* A number of years previous she had read a small paperback book about the rigors of early missionary work in West Africa. Alice could only relate to the fact that 7 out of 10 missionary recruits died within one year of setting foot on Liberian soil. To their credit they never tried to dissuade us from the course of action which we felt was divinely ordained.

We began to divest ourselves from the responsibilities of the church and bade a heart-tugging farewell in November. Congregations all over Alberta began to equip us with linens, household items, canned goods and various other items with which to begin our new venture in Tchien, Liberia. The word "overwhelming" does little to express our emotions as we packed the steel barrels which would carry the gifts across the Atlantic. Once they were securely packed they were soldered shut—to prevent curious thugs from being tempted to pilfer. Looking back on the amount of precious items we felt we could not live without I admit we erred a great deal. Did I really need the gorgeous crystal stem ware (sentimentalized wedding gifts)? The seven pair of sandals? Probably not. Folks kept giving and we kept stuffing the barrels. True, many items were destined to be given out to the school children and pastors' families. But still, I wonder about the abundance....

Given the actuality their only child with their only grandchild were going so far away, it was no wonder their hearts were crushed beyond depth. This is the stuff of nightmares for me. I could not-- WOULD NOT—be so brave and complacent to what was considered "the will of God". A whole lot of howlin' would have filled the night air. And the day air also. Brave hearts indeed.

The shadow side of that pastoral experience gave us both a dimension of depth and maturity we had heretofore not owned. Slowly and methodically the painting was progressing. Oil (think of the symbolic reference of the Holy Spirit) was carefully rubbed in a circular motion. Any excess was removed with a sweeping action of the hand. The discretion of the Master dictated the movement and amount of the oil. The result was a matte finish, smooth and thin with a slight trace of absorbency. A perfect base for future colour.

Liberian Years of Ministry

THE UNCHOREOGRAPHED FAREWELLS were over, final papers signed and our family of three was airborne. An overnight stopover at Heathrow, London prepped us for the final stretch of our sojourn. A quick refueling in Tenerife, Canary Islands heightened the anticipation. A spectacular view of the African continent 25,000 feet below our flight path, made breathing a discipline.

We stepped off the Sabina Airliner at Robertsfield International Airport in Monrovia into a massively dissimilar world to that which we were accustomed—climate, culture, emotional and physical disorientation. The heat rising from the tarmac felt as though bronzing eyeballs was part of its duty.

The first few days we stayed with veteran missionaries who apparently missed the meaning of hospitality. Naturally we were travel stung---weary from the long flight and not quite adapted to the 8 hour time change. We were informed breakfast was served at 7:30 sharp—tardiness was not allowed as both hosts had other duties which made promptness a must. The guest room was small but adequate. The window was laced with iron bars to discourage "rogues". New vocabulary here---what were rogues, pray tell? Large rats? Roving hyenas, perhaps? Deaf elephants? None of the above as it turned out. Common thieves! The word soon became part of our day to day lexicon.

A Portrait in Progress

Orientation had begun.

The country of Liberia was established in 1847 by slaves liberated by the American Revolution. Strong economic ties and overt affection kept both countries attached to each other in ways that are difficult to explain. The descendants of those initial immigrants, known as Americo-Liberians, were generally more educated and well-off than the general indigenous population. Tension between the two groups was never far underground.

American currency was widely used. In the latter part of the late sixties, the Canadian dollar was almost on par with the greenback, 98 cents for every 100 American cents. Tight budgets brought forth grumbles and complaints as in *"Why* can't the Overseas Mission Department compensate us the 2 per cent"? All futile fussing, of course. We would rejoice if those numbers were contemporary!

Our mission was tethered to the American counterpart, the Assemblies of God. Canadian expatriates had to contend with differences in north/south thinking, Adding an extra layer of interest was the movement toward nationalization, a process not unlike the throes of childbirth. Every country, every mission organization faces this type of transition. The black brethren wanted total control of financial matters but were unwilling and ill prepared to assume responsibility for the management of the schools, clinics and necessary in-field training.

After several years of contentious meetings it was decided to transfer the financial accounts on a "let's see what happens" trial basis. What happened was total chaos!! The missionary salaries along with all the teachers and miscellaneous workers were not paid for 3 months. Naturally this was bad news for everyone. Interior Liberia was a "cash only" society. Jess was unable to pay the young men he had as ground maintenance workers, gasoline for the generators and vehicles was running low, teachers were refusing to come to their classrooms etc.

Late one evening a haggard looking Jess told me we had a debt of $1,500 hanging over our heads. It might as well have been $200,000. Before a complete meltdown took us out of range, we decided the only way to manage the situation was to ask for a loan from a cousin. Confidentiality was important. We did not want our friends and supporters in Canada to believe we were working in an untenable situation. The Overseas Mission Department was aware of the circumstances, but seemed unable to offer practical support.

I crafted a letter which gave meager details and laid little responsibility on the national situation. Then we prayed, fervently, that the underlying message would be understood. Less than three weeks later (remarkable in the reality that our mail was delivered once a week in an airdrop) we had a money order which was duly cashed and ended our particular crisis. The letter which accompanied it stated it was a GIFT, not a loan. Can you imagine the joyful gratitude?

I am not sure how the other missionary staff solved their money squeeze. Recalling the anxious weeks from this time frame initiates a wave of sadness. Shortly thereafter the national church decided it was "too troublesome" to manage the accounts, and things returned to normal. Sort of. Annual conferences between all sectors often dissolved into acrimony and fearsome innuendo. This deportment was not solely directed against the missionaries. Raw tribalism raised its ugly specter often as the leaders quarreled amongst themselves.

In addition to teaching health in the elementary school and biblical subjects in the pastoral department, my duties included a makeshift back piazza clinic. Malaria remedies, deworming potions and wound dressings were common requests. My midwifery skills came in handy on a number of occasions. Any help I could offer was greatly appreciated.

Pharmaceuticals of all descriptions (including narcotics and antibiotics) were easily available from corner drug shops run by unscrupulous non-professionals. These medications were often administered by untrained "nurses" who relied more on imagination than information. Creative "recipes" were often injected. There were times when I had to deal with the hideous side effects. One memorable incident—a student who had a seeping open wound allowed a pseudo-nurse to directly inject a syringeful of lemon extract (Watkins Brand was popular at the time!) and penicillin into it. The young man went out of his mind.

The women's groups were outstanding in their zeal to provide care packages for us as well as the student families. We learned to love palm butter, rice and greens, but every once in awhile an urge for authentic Canadian maple syrup, black licorice and canned salmon became an unrepressed whine. Tucked in between layettes school supplies and other sundry items, we would discover treats like these articles. Someone was listening!

One afternoon I unpacked a parcel from church in Saskatchewan. The dear souls had included a large can of salmon, caught off the Pacific coast of B.C.. Somehow reading those words on the label made me sentimental. I decided I would make a casserole the following evening, set out candles and whip up a cake. When I looked for the can of salmon, behold, IT WAS NOT THERE. For one instant I thought the humidity had caused some kind of dementia. Then I remembered folks who lose their minds don't realize that fact. So-o-o another situation presented itself. I gathered up the kitchen trash and headed out to the deep pit where garbage was placed. A heavy cement lid covered it so neither beast nor person could retrieve anything. I found the missing can hidden behind some bushes close by. I walked back to the house with a heavy heart because of the obvious thievery. When questioned about the odd resting place, the girl who was helping me confessed. It was too much of a temptation when her family was begging her to bring something home from the "rich people."

It was not a requirement to learn an entirely new language as by law all educational institutes were to be governed in English. Canadian ears had to undergo an "aural adjustment" in order to process a form of fractured English endearingly referred to as "Liberian English". The first few months were spent plowing through merry mix-ups as I tried to maintain a veneer of dignity at the same time feeling terribly dumb.

Flat tire***The foot is broken and the breeze has moved.
Labour (maternity)***Her belly is doing her.
No responsibility***My hand not inside it.

Smart person***She talk big with small words.
Disappointment***My heart fell down.
Hunger***Empty bag cannot stand.
Smile***Laugh small.
Letter closing before signature***Stifling with affection.
I will think about it****I will hang head.
Dysentery***His stomach is running.

From time to time visitors came from "home countries" wanting to help in ministry or other tasks. Most of them were a joy to have around. Sometimes it was difficult to get accustomed to the climate and routines in a short period of time. One memorable pastor preached a worthy sermon on God's provision. He used food as the over-riding example. Unfortunately he missed the point as he kept mentioning bacon, pancakes and maple syrup, The confused interpreter, familiar with only rice and palm butter, kept translating the monologue as "chop chop". One very rotund gentleman kept his audience awake by trying to figure out how many cups of rice he ate every day. A young youth pastor took a liking to one of our Liberian students which went far beyond a suitable evangelical passion for her soul.

Naturally communication became muddled more times than believable. I have jagged memories of trying to help the school girls who worked for us understand the simplest tasks. We paid their tuition and provided some of their uniforms. Most of them were eager and industrious. One wash day Victoria used furniture polish in the final rinse instead of fabric softener. All garments and linens were air dried under a hot tin car port which made softness a wild fantasy. Thus the need for a bit of luxury. That day we had the shiniest sheets on the compound. Another afternoon as I was trying to assist the pastoral students in their understanding of parasites, Martha bathed the twins—a step of trust on my part if there ever was one. As a finishing touch she slathered cough syrup on their heads thinking it was hair dressing. Esther "anointed" the walls of the laundry room one morning with kerosene, positive I had purchased a new kind of cleaner. Do I need to mention company was almost at the door when I discovered that blunder? Kerosene fumes are not an easy smell to eradicate quickly!!!

Communicating with twisted jargon became second nature after a few months. I suppose its nuances also slipped into our written missives to supporting churches. One central B.C. Church was most generous with gifts of complete layettes for the babies born to our pastors and teachers. Actually, any woman who showed up on our piaaza with a newborn was gladly given one. My letter of thanks to the women's group who had collected and sent the parcels was thoughtful and heartfelt. So I thought, until I received a letter in response. The main message was, *"We could not understand what you were saying and writing about. Perhaps we should not communicate with you again."* I was thoroughly stung as I could not imagine what had been written that was so offensive. Never heard from them again.

Having house help was an important part of our ministry, as odd as that sounds. It helped dissipate rumours that missionaries were hiding hordes of clothes, food, money. We wanted to become more familiar with the common idioms and customs of the people to which we were called to minister. In addition, valuable lessons could be learned by watching a Christian marriage in action. Our home had Joliffe windows—glass slates that could be moved up or down like Venetian blinds. Every day reddish dust billowed up the mission hill as the logging trucks lumbered their way towards the coast. Time pressure made it impossible to dust every day however badly the need presented itself. I felt I was not called to Africa to be immersed in endless washing, dusting and disinfecting.

Jess supervised the building of our cement block house. He was precise in nature. His construction workers were not. The nightmares he had with unskilled labourers who were adept at combining sloth with dishonesty are worth a book in themselves. Time was not an important aspect of their value system. The men worked hard in the heat and under the "along side supervision" of Pa Lynn. Nevertheless, the day after we had enjoyed a brief vacation away from the building site, a serious error had occurred in our absence. The walls were several degrees "off" which meant the roof would be slightly askew forever.

Because of the duress of other duties, the kitchen cupboards were without doors for 2 years which precipitated an inordinate amount of stress. The floors were bare cement with white-washed walls. Practical and livable. One Christmas, in an expression of devoted love, Jess paneled a bare wall in the living room with a variety of indigenous woods that were considered unfit for export by a nearby European lumber establishment. He cut, sanded and varnished for days. The result was worth it! It lifted the house into a new level. I knew the sacrifices in time and effort he had made. I felt loved every time I passed that way. When the civil war began in 1980, our house was used by the rebels for a shelter. The feature wall was ripped out and used as firewood.

Annie Cressman was a dedicated soul who came to Liberia in the early forties. Difficult to imagine the extraordinary circumstances which she overcame to become fluent in the Tchien dialect. She was beloved by ex-pats as well as the nationals. Her grace and patience were legendary. She was a repository of knowledge about everything Liberian. We were blessed to have her friendship and help during our formative years in a new setting.

One of the regrettable lapses in our "school of missions" tutelage was the lack of discussion around ethical issues. For instance, most Christians have been taught that bribery is a vice (SIN, perhaps) to be avoided at all costs. However, in Liberia, bribery was a way of life. An ex-pat, regardless of status, could have a life or schedule totally disrupted if this custom was ignored. A police officer could stop a motorist for any confabulated reason and demand a court appearance. A five dollar bill placed in the driver's license would bring a smile and the absolution of the non-crime.

One time I was stopped by a gun-toting police officer who shouted at me the headlights were blinking alternatively. This was an impossibility with the particular Peugeot I was driving. I told him nicely I didn't think that was possible, but please, could we talk further? He snorted and continued on in a frightful fashion. I had no way of informing my husband I could be delayed for hours or even days if this idiotic exchange continued. Our children were being cared for by another missionary family and heaven knew how much a lawyer would cost to pursue this event in court. I slipped him a battered five buck bill and inwardly moaned as he wished me a pleasant day. Some expatriates would view this type of resolution as tantamount to a mortal sin, and refuse to succumb under any circumstances. Those folks had a lot of stress-related diseases and many wasted hours.

Another missionary whose nationality was not from the true north, strong and free made a scene about us eating kola nuts. The tradition in some of the backcountry areas was to offer guests the bitter, claret-coloured nuts as a gesture of welcoming hospitality. Did we not realize they were...ADDICTIVE???? The scalding taste did wonders to prevent such a condition from developing, trust me. As a matter of interest, this same gentleman, by his own blush-free admission, drank six cans of Coca Cola daily. So the question presented itself with clarity—who was the one with the problem??!!

We kept cats to discourage mice and their big cousins, rats. That was the solitary reason. Never was infected with feline fancy. To my regret, one homely tabby drove me within a hair's distance of murder. Is felinecide a word that is in common use? One sweltering afternoon, after destroying an artful dessert I had carefully prepared for guests and then mutilating a couple of chicken breasts, I wrapped her/him in an elderly pillowcase and attempted to drown him/her in the rain barrel. The howls which ensued during this primitive water-boarding coerced me into shame and I yanked it out. The terrifying experience must have triggered an aqua-memory lapse as two days later the creature was back on the piazza expecting chow. Seems to me I remember a rash later that evening. I repaired the dessert by scooping out the paw prints and adding another layer of custard. The chicken breasts were dissected in such a clever manner no one could have guessed their previous fate. Remedial actions such as these examples are known as 'coping management"! They happened frequently.

In December 1969, Jess and I knew our family was on the increase. We just didn't know by how much! I didn't get too concerned about finding a doctor until late February. A Baptist Mission about 2 hours distance away was my first thought. After the doctor examined me he told me regretfully he could not deliver me as he was only "allowed to help Liberian women." We drove home in a state of angry shock. How far was that from high-grade idiocy? The next option was an international lumber operating near Cape Palmas, a 5 hour motor trip away. The staff was sympathetic to us, but under company rules only employees and their families could be serviced. This was getting serious. The due date was in July, smack in the middle of rainy season when often the dirt road was closed because of washouts. That meant the Methodist Hospital in Ganta, (4 hours away) was a risky option. It was tempting to proceed into panic mode, but we were learning. Keep calm and call on God.

The pregnancy was a bit different than my first. I was ill, could not stand the smell or taste of rice (positively awful when rice is the main diet staple!) and getting rounder than I liked. All these signs should have triggered a brain wave or at the very least an epiphany. Providentially, the fact that it was a multiple pregnancy, was totally outside the realm of my consciousness. A very loving provision on the part of God. Had I suspected twins were the reason I felt a flamingo dance competition was held daily in my tummy, I would have come apart emotionally.

Not wanting to alarm my parents too much, I wrote and invited them to double (HA!) their prayers for a miracle. They canceled their planned trip to Liberia and sent the money for Regan and myself to fly home. Jess was unable to get permission to accompany us. Oh well...

Before the final preparations were made for the flight to Edmonton, we discussed names for this new addition. We thought it wise to have TWO sets of names just in case... a joke of course. That TEE HEE was about to morph into "Oh my goodness" in less than a week.

We booked a Pan Am flight early in May. I required a letter from a qualified medical person stating I was healthy enough to fly. Arrangements were made to stop in Ganta on our way to the airport. Jess stayed with Regan in the courtyard as I waited for document. The doctor did his due diligence and while I was still on the examining table, I heard him breathe a soft hmmm-m. Ever hear a mechanic do that while peering at an engine taken in for repair? An approximate translation is " I've found something unusual here". What the doctor actually said was "Either you have a two headed monster here, or you are carrying twins!"

Good thing I was lying down. Suddenly it was hard to breathe but easy to laugh! The missing piece snapped into position and the puzzle was solved. How could have I missed all the obvious signs? Telling Jess was fun! He turned pale, coughed and sputtered "Lets get something to eat!". The news lightened our last 2 days together. We snickered over how to tell the news to our co-workers and parents. More sobering though, was the thought of doubling all the infant necessities.

With some difficulty I walked up the stairs into the plane. The flight attendant took one look at me and asked rather incredulously, *"My, my and what do we have here? A mama elephant?"* I can only imagine I must have wobbled as I steered my small son in front of me trying to balance carry-on luggage and remain upright. London meant a brief stopover, but I was not worried. Lots of staff to help us get through the holding area and find our Canadian airline. Just as we were landing, the pilot made an announcement *"Ladies and gentleman, I am sorry to inform you 5 minutes ago a wildcat strike was called. There will be no ground staff to assist you in any way".* A corporate groan filled the air. Jolly good. Just what the doctor ordered.

Somehow a portion of grace was granted us and without a recordable incident we touched down in Edmonton's International Airport unscathed. Grampa and Gramma Thompson were thrilled beyond words to hold and hug Regan. They were not quite so ecstatic about the twin news. My mother started to cry. "How in the world will you manage?" she said, clearly conveying her anxiety for my well-being. Well, I couldn't answer with any great assurance, but I knew I would get the strength, enough and on time!

The two months we lived with my parents before the arrival of the babies was a godsend all around. I rested while the grandparents learned first hand how energetic little lads are. I spoke at several ladies groups and gathered clothes and essentials for all of us. The ob-gyn doctor I chose was Dr. David Reid. I knew him from my days in the University Hospital's obstetrical ward. The expected date of confinement was mid-July. Multiple births usually deliver early, so I began to petition the universe for a July 1st birthing day. I thought it would be a recompense seeing I loved my country so much. It would be great sport to tease my America friends also. The day previous to Canada Day 1970 I wore myself out ---shopping with Norma who was also expecting. All the effort was for nought. We shopped until we dropped, but the babies did not! Then I began praying I would not go into labour until after July 4th. That was for nought also! Early on the morning of the fourth of July, the twins were knocking on the door. My father was terrified they would announce themselves in his Chevrolet if he drove over a bump of any size. As a result of the slow-motion drive to the hospital I was in full labour! The babies were delivered, both a good weight. Their daddy did not know about their arrival until 2 days later due to communication difficulties. Our America friends teased us forever over what they considered poetic justice.

The congregation of Edmonton Central Tabernacle went beyond expectations in their love and caring for us. My mom took Renard as her special charge. She rocked him to sleep when I was busy with his brother. With her assistance I learned how to breast feed both at one time—a time saver of the utmost importance. I made the decision to remain in Canada until the babies were 2 and ½ months old. We flew to Ontario to spend a week with Jess's parents who were home on furlough. It was time to introduce the infants to bottle feeding. They were unimpressed. My mother-in-law and Aunt Marion Lynn (Kenneth's mother!) were an enormous help in the transition. They figured if they were hungry enough they would stop their shrieking and at least lick the new nipple out of curiosity. It worked! Four days later they were weaned and we were ready to take off.

Early in the morning of our schedule flight to Liberia, I did a final check to make sure everything was in order. Several suitcases were loaded with gifts and goodies. Previous to this date I had double checked to make sure an infant car bed would be accommodated on the flight. Yes, indeed. No problem. A lesson in checking out assumptions was on the horizon. I packed plenty of cloth diapers and clothes under the mattress plus anything else "skinny" which I thought might come in handy before reaching our destination.

A diligent search did not reveal the important health booklets which recorded our immunizations necessary for travel abroad. I knew they were someplace as we had had them updated a few days before. They were nowhere to be found. This necessitated an early rushed trip to Toronto's Pearson Airport to be re-immunized for a couple of obligatory doses. Naturally this did not make for a relaxed pre-flight experience. Edna Lynn traveled along with me to New York's Kennedy Airport where another adventure was about to unfold. She was a wonderful help with the children. When we said good bye in the holding area I felt a sense of despair. All the responsibility to get the four of us back to Liberia was mine alone.

We had several hours to wait before the flight to Monrovia . I had a twitch of anxiety when the gate looked at me quizzically and noted I had 3 children traveling with me. Kindly she explained an adult could only travel with one infant only---safety regulations. Furthermore, how did I get here anyhow? I needed to proceed to Pan Am's airport headquarters and check this out. She suggested I locate someone close by to mind the sleeping twins while I made the journey through the airport to straighten out this dilemma. I had already made the acquaintance of a missionary couple on their way back to West Africa, so I felt at ease leaving them. I grabbed Regan's hand and ran out to find the office. The stress stuff was starting to show. By now my oldest son was thirsty, so I stopped at a booth to get him some pop. The clerk threw back my Canadian quarter (those were the days..!) with a snarly "We don't accept foreign money." Jeepers!! Before I could come back with a witty repartee, a gentleman close by handed me an American quarter and we were on our way. The kindness of strangers. The office staff offered me no assistance, but at least they shrugged and allowed us to fly regardless.

Upon our arrival back in the holding area, the atmosphere had changed. Passengers were crying. Some were pacing. All looked stricken. A newly airborne plane, on its way to pick up a full load of passengers,had crashed at the end of a runway. The smoke and flames were visible from the windows in our area. To expedite the investigation the entire airport was shut down for eight hours. If I remember correctly the airline brought in food for the passengers as the hours wore on. My biggest worry? I had brought only enough formula to last the trans-Atlantic flight! I kept thinking about Christ feeding the 5,000 and wondered if my family could apply for a similar miracle. The gate staff changed during the unscheduled delay. The new agent noticed the car bed and questioned me about it. She told me it definitely was NOT ALLOWED. I would have to check it in, which meant another trot back to the check in place. By this time I am weary, and just a touch cranky. Nothing to do except leave the kids with this trusted couple and make a marathon dash back to the check in counter. Which I did in record time. I know this was a long time ago, but still---were phones not available to spare the agony? When I returned it was time to board.

All fastened in and taxiing down the runway. At last I could relax. Not so fast. The next thought yanked my delusion away. In my haste to comply with the admonition to check the car bed, I forgot the extra diapers and formula were tucked under the linen. A trans-Atlantic flight with hungry, poopy babies? Lord, have mercy. Once the seatbelt sign was turned off, I mentioned my problem to one of the flight attendants.

"Oh, no problem" she assured me. For 3 minutes I relaxed. Then she re-appeared with a frown. OOPS. Big problem. With the chaos that had erupted after the tragedy, the usual baby supply kit had been left behind. I figured I was doomed. It was one of those times—the best and the worst—that people like me need a miracle. Two or three would be better. First I implored the Lord to make Regan very sleepy. Then I asked that the 2% milk I had to feed the twins would taste like

Nestle's formula. Finally I begged that the immigration officials would not notice the health booklets were incomplete as the yellow fever shot could not be repeated in Toronto. When the twins need a change of diaper the flight attendant procured several first class napkins which did the trick. Soft, but not entirely absorbent.

The aircraft touched down on time, I marched bravely in, remembering my prayer. I added an addendum—make the twinnies cry so the officers will be distracted. I waved to Jess through the glass doors and Regan ran to greet his Daddy. Right on cue Renard and Rael began to holler. The inspector looked at me and said"Yours?". "Yes, Sir". Under my breath it was "bought and paid for". He waved me through with a brisk "Go". The end of the story? Not quite. Three weeks later a bulky brown envelope arrived. It contained the four international health booklets! My mother-in-law, Edna Lynn, with her sense of organization, had taken them in an act of gracious well-meaning and stored them in her purse. The purse which incidentally she was carrying the day she traveled with me. I tried to laugh but a frown kept getting in its way. Good story for years to come!

The arrival of our twins seemed to inaugurate a spate of multiple births. A number of colleagues and national pastors' wives gave birth to sets of twins, and we were "blamed". I was granted 6 months of teaching free time once I returned with the children. It was not long enough.

One morning I was summoned to the office of the District Superintendent, Colonel White. The position was the equivalent of a provincial premier or governor. The request was hand delivered by a messenger in a chauffeur-driven Mercedes Benz.

One the small talk formalities end, I was informed I had been "chosen"to direct a choir of 100 school children in a musical selection for the upcoming celebration of the nation's independence. The president of the Liberia would be in attendance along with foreign dignitaries. President Tolbert had decreed the "Hallelujah Chorus" was to be performed.

I remember feeling dizzy and wanting to offer some excuse with some metaphysical trappings. Executive protocol precludes that option. Dealing with that particular governing administration was somewhat like dealing with the Almighty. You did what was declared or died in the attempt.

Let me elucidate the details. These children came from an indigenous culture whose music was totally in minor keys. Their attendance on school days depended on the presence of the rice harvest or the absence of malaria. In three words--unreliable at best. The fact they could not read music notations was immaterial as there was no music sheets for them to read! Only two copies of the composition were available, one for the director, the other for the pianist. My accompanist was a pregnant teacher in her first trimester who had the unfortunate malady of morning-all-day sickness. Rehearsals were the only times she stopped throwing up.

For the first few weeks we had neither piano nor pianist. Each part had to be taught separately. Getting the altos, tenors and basses to sit quietly while I drilled the sopranos was a feat memorable. Many times I blessed Handel for the wisdom of simple lyrics. A Liberian teacher usually sat in the room with the children, bellowing out threats in dialect when he saw mischief percolating.

I cried every day for weeks. The choir was a *dumb* idea in my opinion. My equipoise was seared every time I contemplated the command performance. My prayers for a merciful intervention were miraculously answered when another appointment was scheduled with Colonel White. He hasten to inform me I had done an admirable job under the wearisome circumstances, thank you very much. *However,* word had been received that President Tolbert was dismayed a white woman was directing the choir. I never figured out which concept bothered him the most, white or woman. Nevertheless, I was replaced by a black, male musician.

The gentleman was an elderly bundle of musical genius. He was the grandson of repatriated American slaves. Mr. Grant's forte was perfect pitch. He was raised on a mission compound near the Ivory Coast border. When he was in elementary school he would sneak into

A Portrait in Progress

the chapel and despite threat of severe discipline, sit down at the piano and compose melodies. The principal of the school finally realized this barefoot child of the rain forest was divinely blessed with rare musical ability. The youngster was allowed special privileges and given the best musical training available.

In a matter of weeks he had subdued those students by fierce yelling in an unknown tongue and waving his baton close to their heads. When the celebration day arrived, they were *ready*. I stood near the back of the auditorium and listened with tears hovering on the edge. They never missed a beat and were only slightly off-key. The passage of years does nothing to mute the memory.

The pace never seemed to lessen. If my family was to be clothed, I had to sew. Economics decreed that state of affairs. The entry of June 29, 1971 gives an indication of the pressure.

> *Had a high fever again today.. I'm beginning to wonder if it may be infectious hepatitis. Hope not. Cut out blue blouse and orange dress --sewed like mad in the p.m.*

My husband spent more time repairing lawnmowers than I care to remember. It became a source of frustration that sometimes grew to seething anger. To this very day, whenever I see a LawnBoy mower, I have a sudden rush of revenge which makes me want to kick it. Goats seemed like an ideal solution. When we considered the fact they would be prime objects for theft, the decision was "not at this time". One bleak evening, a full moon gracing an ink black sky, I sat on the front steps, and prayed for strength to run away. The cool gentle breeze helped me regain my senses.

In December of 1974 I began to experience an urge to adopt a baby girl. This was a puzzlement as the 3 boys were a satisfying handful. The sensation was so overwhelming I discussed it at length with Jess as well as a colleague. When I returned to Edmonton a few years later I consulted with the doctor who had delivered Renard and Rael. He offered very little hope because I had 3 children already. At that time a wait of

10 years was common. I laid the dream down, rationalizing it had been an emotional fantasy. Writing and researching a Master's thesis in 1999 offered me the grace of an epiphany. The urge had come around the same time my birth father lay dying in a northern B.C. Hospital.

One of the dismal aches many missionary parents live with is the necessity to send their youngsters to boarding school. We enrolled Regan in an excellent Baptist school, 600 kilometers away in neighboring Ivory Coast. In August of 1976 his brothers joined him. We steeled our hearts and prayed they would adjust to the school routine as well as dormitory life. The kids were only six. How did we do it? To this day I cannot tell you. At the time it seemed like the only option.

My sons' memories of those early school days are muffled. Perhaps repressed. On quiet days I berate myself for putting them in that situation. They were well prepared for the Canadian school system when we returned which was a cornerstone in the decision. The fact Jess spent most of his schooling in Kenya's Rift Valley Academy helped us accept the fact. The school year was divided into 3 month semesters. Parents were not allowed to visit their children during that time, even if they lived several kilometers away. It was deemed to be a fair system.

I enrolled in a correspondence writing course to stave off the empty house blues. It didn't work! I honed my writing skills and decided someday when the opportunity presented itself, I would write. Stories, newspaper columns, humour features, whatever.

In the spring of '77 our hearts turned toward home. Extra duties had been handed to us. As we pushed ourselves to the edge of total exhaustion, the thought of never returning became more alluring. Our plans were formulated on the premise we would leave as soon as the final semester of the boarding school ended. On April 13 , I scribbled this cranky entry into my journal.

> *I just decided to SHELVE the idea of a form letter telling everyone we are homeward bound, even tho' it is an expected duty!!! Only one of us is going home a WRECK from ill-placed priorities!!!*

A Portrait in Progress

We began to question our future with the Overseas Mission Department. Generally we felt disheartened with mission life. Sending the 3 Rs to school in the Ivory Coast meant constant hassles at the border. Had there been a coup in either country, passage across to retrieve our sons may have been impossible.

My parents were aging. As an only child I felt responsible in large measure for their well-being. Financially, we were depleted. The country was in a pre-revolutionary state with anti-white sentiment on the increase. We grew abundantly disillusioned with the Liberian leadership's motives and methods. Weary of some of our own colleagues attitudes, we flew home waving a definite maybe.

Hindsight, with its ultimate clarity, informs me those years were pivotal in shaping me for future ministry. Our mandate was to teach the people to whom we had been called, employing precept as well as modeling biblical living. In the end, they taught us life lessons which endure to this day. The following are examples of the gifts they unknowingly gave us.

Attitudes regarding—

1. Hospitality, as opposed to entertainment. The most memorable meal I ever had was during the season of hunger, a period of 4-5 weeks before the rice harvest began. Deep into the forest we drove, then walked a short distance to a nicely kept mud-plastered hut. My hostess apologized she had no meat to serve me. Supper consisted of a small bowl of fluffy rice doused with orange-red palm oil. Nothing else, but this was offered with a willing heart while her family probably had less. This is the essence of hospitality. An African proverb puts it another way—*if you don't share , you will choke*. I think with fondness the time Larry and Doreen Broughton had the good fortune to procure a small bunch of luscious green grapes during a grocery trip 450 Kms away. It was a big event to snag such a rare treat. Doreen invited us over and laid out her best dishes. On each of them lay four grapes—our individual portion from their cache. She informed us she was sharing because

she knew we LOVED grapes. It was a sacrifice on their part because of the atrocious price. Our mutual laughter made them so much sweeter.

2. The inescapable fact of death. There were no funeral parlours or coffins draped with satin to distract mourners from the finality of death. They viewed life as a cycle which happened to everyone. Burials were within two days due to the climate. "Life must go on" was a mantra. Sometimes when a husband was deep in a coma, relatives freely conversed about who his widow should marry, and the sooner the better. This always struck a melancholy chord with me. I have had a couple of occasions to recall this custom! No such thing as convoluted, pathological grief which was sustained for years after a death.

3. Resilience. Tribal tensions, childbirth horror stories, crop failures leading to near starvation, diseases, the like of which North Americans have never seen, successive governments incompetence, on and on. The citizens have survived, raised families and sent their gratitude heavenward. There were times we felt we were there for 8 years working on a thousand year project.

4. Stress Management Education---by osmosis! Explanation of this phenomena is futile. All I can say is by the time we set foot back in Canada I had an understanding of stress and its effects. No books, magazines, audio tapes, TV series—I just had a Holy Spirit course which equipped me to minister to individuals who were trying to understand how stress in their lives was causing them DISTRESS. The late seventies spawned books by researchers who made a connection between stress and the body's reaction. This was a new way looking at mind-body connection. I eagerly read everything about the subject I laid my hands on. The intriguing part was I already knew what these authors were talking about even though I had NO access to previous material. Liberia was my "greening time" for a new avenue of ministry that was just over the hill.

These gifts were not overspread with shiny tissue held together with glistening silk ties. Neither were they delivered on special celebration days. Often they were unheralded, misunderstood and rejected, until at a later date their value was revealed.

This next stage of a painting is known as "dead colouring". It does not involve a casual laying down of subdued colours. Rather, the artist reflects on the future of the painting. He anticipates the colours in relation to the later stages of the work. The colours used in the "dead colouring" must have a purpose. Any areas that are to be painted white can be placed at this stage in the shadows. When this period of preparation is complete the portrait is set aside for a specific time to dry. It needs to rest before further work is commenced.

The Wainwright Saga

OUR FAMILY WAS only home for a few months when a decisive "no, we do not plan on returning" became part of our daily conversations. The first priority was finding a house to rent for a year until our obligation with the Mission Department was complete. We were offered a pleasant house in a new subdivision. The kind owners accepted the amount ($365.00 monthly) stipulated by head office. In reality, that couple suffered a loss because the average rent for an equitable dwelling was much higher. Riverbend Elementary School was 3 blocks away. Perfect.

We settled into a domestic routine which was characterized by Jess's frequent absences as he traveled the Western provinces promoting the work of missions. The children adjusted well to the Edmonton Public School system, Regan in grade 5 while Renard and Rael toiled along in grade 2.

I knew nursing was part of who I was. In the early months of 1978 I renewed my R.N. registration by completing a stiff refresher course at the University Hospital. Traveling by transit bus every weekday to classes and clinical experience was an odyssey of discomfort. Nursing had changed significantly in attitude and technology. Street terminology had shifted also.

I was assigned to a major medical floor. One of the patients at the end of the hallway was a nurse who had graduated two years ahead of me. In my memory she was a beautiful, talented young woman, loved by all who knew her. I recognized her name on the cardex, but she was not one of my patients. She lay comatose as a result of an aggressive cranial cancer. When I mentioned I knew her as an upper class member years ago, a young nurse piped up and said, "*Too bad, she's a dork now.*" It was an unfortunate moment to allow my ignorance to squeak out by inquiring " *What is a DORK?*" I was answered with a scalding look that burns me to this day.

A defining moment occurred during the lecture on obstetrics. The tall, assertive instructor talked about the latest technology used in modern labor and delivery suites. The nurses could sit in the central office space and decide the status of mother and baby by means of internal fetal monitors. A computer readout showed the progress of labor. No comforting breath coach or doula to encourage the moms. A shocking revelation for one trained in the "old school" of personal presence. The appeal of detailed statistics did not dissuade me from changing direction in regard to future nursing choices. Geriatrics became my passion.

When an itinerating missionary safaris around the country promoting overseas projects, s/he has the dubious opportunity (??) to hear about the inner workings of many churches, large, small, urban, rural. The squabbling factions were nearly identical in vice and actions. By the time six months of speaking engagements were over, we had a list of assemblies we knew we did not want to pastor. Our hearts went out to the poor pastoral couple called to lead these awkward congregations. Wainwright, on the eastern border of the sunniest province was on the list. Now, here is a word to the wives---never listen to just one side of any story. People who have issues with the people to whom they are called, often have unresolved issues within themselves.

We had been designated to speak in Wainwright one chilly Sunday in January 1978. Arriving too early for Sunday School, we drove to the pastor's home. The atmosphere in that living room was frosty also, but for a different reason. Rueben didn't mince his words as a torrent of pent-up gall spewed forth. He was exasperated trying to lead the congregation dragging their heels. He told us his plan to resign ---soon. He neglected to tell us HOW soon.

Propped up in the second row from the front, my sons and I settled in for the morning worship service. Jess sat on the platform with the host minister. Just before this pastoral gentleman gave the invocation to worship, he unceremoniously proclaimed, *"As of two weeks from today, I will no longer be your pastor. This is the official announcement of my resignation. Our first hymn is number 152."*

I choked back a cough which threatened to become a titter. A profoundly uninspired service followed, as one can imagine. As the tension grew by the minute I thought *"Horrible church, worse than horrible leadership. Who in their right mind would even consider coming here? Not us. NEVER. Thanks for the warning, Lord."*

In several previous *tete a tetes* with the Almighty we had requested a CHURCH, not a challenge, to shepherd. We thought our petition was clear and and unequivocal. Behold, it is never too early to learn that holding up a preconceived agenda to God and asking for Divine approval is not a particularly witty course of action. During the drive back home, the three kids asleep, Jess and I had a long, lucid conversation. As we parked in the driveway, we both agreed that if the board of elders "called" us, we would be MORE THAN THRILLED to answer in the affirmative. Please do not ask me to explain! In less time it takes to make an appointment for an engine overhaul, a letter arrived requesting us to consider coming to Wainwright as pastors. Glory bound!!

Our advent in rural Alberta followed an 11 year association with our denomination's Overseas Mission Department. In Liberia our students were pastors and their people who were thrilled with the rudimentary stories and principles of the Bible. They listened, believed and carried the precepts back to their villages sometimes trekking for hours through uncut jungle growth.

The congregation to which we were called had a long history. No doubt over the years, the members had heard every angle possible on justification, working out a personal salvation, lessons from the Feast of Tabernacles and frightening end time scenes from the book of

Revelation. It was difficult to present something old in new packaging and still keep the integrity of truth. Various translations of the Bible caused minor rifts, as in *"What version did the pastor use today?,*

We wanted to purchase a house. Parsonage living was not an attractive option. The board of elders were progressive thinkers. Suggesting a loan of $15,000 as a down payment made it easy for us to house-hunt. I prayed for trees, a garden, a family room, 2 bathrooms and a suitable guestroom in addition to all the usual requests. One afternoon we drove down to view a house that was for sale, but not yet on the market. Walking in the front door convinced me our search was over. I did not need to waste the rest of the afternoon looking at houses that I knew were...unsuitable! We negotiated a mortgage for a rate of 13 ½ percent. It was considered a bargain . Not many months later some co-workers and friends were struggling with rates that had climbed to 15-18 %.

The neigbourhood was a microcosm of the town—the world maybe. Across the street lived a husband whose wife had a tryst with a local funeral director. The enraged gentleman rewarded the lover with a prominent black eye and a wounded soul. What kind of explanation was given the next day to grieving relatives at a solemn funeral? Too bad I wasn't present.

Our little house on 2nd Avenue was a perfect answer to prayer. The back platform porch was showing its age, but that was part of its charm. I secured a part-time R.N. position in the Auxiliary Hospital which helped lessen the constant stress about finances. We were blessed numerous times in unexpected ways. I believe the term "miracle" is appropriate here. Each spring and summer I endeavoured to create an oasis of sight and fragrance on the deck. One season I toured all the greenhouses in the area, gathering as much greenery and blooms as I dared. My wallet was several hundred dollars lighter (a sum to be defined as outrageous!) when I finished arranging my bounty. To my husband's credit, he did not inquire the cost of such beauty. To my credit, I did not inform him! It seemed to me the luxury of the planters outweighed the leanness of Kraft Dinner for many suppers in a row.

The beauty of nature was a "shout out" to the Creator's bounty. I adopted that as my mantra whenever I felt a tickle of guilt. Of course there are times when hard, cold cash is needed to make such a situation a reality. After a gentle rain the ambiance of that porch was brushed with an intoxicating fragrance. Sitting on the old-fashioned deck was a lovely respite from the existential angst that always accompanies pastoring and parenting.

The neighbour on the right, Miss Theresa, was the type of lady a family would pay to have her as their Gramma. The neighbour on the other side was the type of man a family would pay him NOT to be their Grampa. Close by folks taught me how to garden, bake old fashioned fruit cakes and which people could be trusted.

It was a very conservative congregation. Two of the charter members were still alive and active. It was a compelling study in ecclesiastical dynamics to observe the patriarchs wrestling power plays from time to time. Even more disturbing was the biting edginess that often accompanied the social interaction of the 2nd and 3rd generations.

One afternoon Jess and I had a quiet argument about money, a perennial thorn in an otherwise rosy relationship. He phoned after stomping over to his office---and I refused to talk to him. Regan, his eyes wide with fearful anticipation, asked if we were going to get a divorce. Jess's methodical mind required each bank statement had to be reconciled to within exact pennies. Such exactness was beyond my capabilities. I was happy if there was a positive balance! My style of dealing with negative emotions (the "stuff and smolder method")was not helpful. I needed to learn how to cope with aggravation in a way that was healthy as well as affirming. Prime chances to do exactly that were looming on the horizon.

The local Home and School Association seemed a fitting organization to lend my strength in the community at large. For two years I was president. It became my contention that Christian parents needed to pull their weight in supporting the the public schools. We could be

A Portrait in Progress

agents of change in meaningful ways. Volunteering instead of sniping could lessen the need for denominational schools. The discussion, pro and con, carried on for months. A vigorous attempt to establish a Christian school in town was widely promoted. I openly opposed it which was considered somewhat blasphemous. At the time funding for education was vastly different than at present. That factor was part of my rationale for a presenting a counterpoint position. In the end, the endeavour came to nought and town life resumed its methodical pace.

One of my responsibilities of church life was the Sunday morning Christian Ed. Class for the youth. Managing last minute details before gathering my sons together and checking if appropriate outfits were in place often meant long delays and short tempers. One morning we were late leaving the house and as I backed out of the garage I ripped off the mirror on the driver's side. Just great. I was forced into guilty silence as we arrived at the church. I was teaching about "patience" that morning, and had just given our kids a very poor example. The next Sunday I determined to do better. The boys were more annoying than precious that day. As I backed the car out, I accidentally rammed into our garden fence, demolishing a couple of boards. I heard a quiet "OOOPS" emanate from the back seat which did nothing to sweeten my mood. I knew my lesson was on loving each other and at that moment I felt like reaching out and touching someone---hard. What hygienic explanation could I think up between the offertory and the benediction?

One evening just as I settled into a quiet mood for reading, I heard one of my sons call from the upstairs bathroom, *"Mom, MOM—please come and see me!",* his voice ragged with anxiety.

> VL. *You are taking a bath. Can it wait until you are finished?*
> RL. *NO! I need to talk to you right now.*

I opened the door and peeked in. A facecloth had been strategically placed. Modesty reigned.

VL. *Is something wrong?*
RL. *Yes! I think I am a mutant!*
VL. *A WHAT?? Whatever happened to make you think that?*
RL. *We-l-l-l, I found 3 hairs in my pubic area and I am worried.*
VL. *Dear Son, You. Are. Normal. Pretty soon you will have 300 more. It is a sign you are growing up.*
RL. *Oh-h-h, well okay then. Thanks. You can go now!*

I leaned against the hallway wall and figured I'd better look up the word mutant in our dictionary. Breathing without giggling was impossible.

Usually a sparkly group which was a joy to teach, in the weeks prior to Christmas 1979, the youth became sullen, sick and tough to teach. They were experiencing pre-festive school stress, but did not have the vocabulary to express it. Reaching back into my own "extracted knowledge" from the Liberian era, I prepared a session on stress management for the next Sunday. It was a sweet revelation to watch the "light bulbs" go on in their heads.

The parents heard about the session and requested I repeat it in the adult class. The topic was an instant success and stretched into 3 sessions. A stroke of luminosity hit me---I knew without a doubt I was onto a great idea. A few weeks later I was asked to speak on the same topic at a Lutheran ladies gathering in a nearby town. VOILA ! Suddenly it was a contemporary subject and no one else in sight was teaching it. The door flew open and I walked through it. An offer from the local Further Education office afforded me the opportunity to set up a 6 week course.

Requests came from a variety of organizations to present similar sessions. The monetary aspect of it proved to be delightful. In 1981 I endeavoured to get a book covering the subject published. *"Life Doesn't Have to be a Pain"* was the proposed title. It was an expansion of some articles I had written for a nurses' magazine some months earlier. Contacting several publishers, I enclosed an outline, a completed first chapter and a suggested conclusion. Heartily rejected by 3 companies, I swallowed my disappointment and vowed to revise and rewrite the manuscript. I kept teaching stress to audiences that were "getting the concept" and applying it to their daily lives. In the autumn of 1982 I eventually discovered my personal "practicum" in stress management was lamentably incomplete.

The summer proved to be lackluster in regards to the church. Nothing untoward was on the horizon, but a feeling of malaise had crept into the atmosphere. Nobody seemed excited about anything, not even the weather. We wondered if our time could be described as treading water---not drowning but not reaching a point of satisfaction either. We received an invitation to pastor a church in Hay River, NWT. For 3 days we were tempted to sign on. Remembering our time spent there years before, tinted our vision. Unexplained, the urge to return shifted. Our spirits were restless until we notified the person in charge we would not be available. We could not figure out why.

The church was relatively stable in the summer of 1982. My partner's health was not. Jess began to notice a disabling lightheadedness whenever he exerted himself—jogging, bike riding and so on. The initial episode occurred as we were biking up a steep hill near our summer cabin. He was right behind as we started the incline, When I reached the top I turned with a little holler of victory. Jess was sitting on the ground, his bike beside him. Rushing back down, I asked him what happened. He passed it off as a silly moment of breathlessness. Together we slowly walked up the hill and rested before heading home. When wrestling with the boys he would cry "uncle" and tell them they were getting way too strong for him.

The malady escalated into periodic blackouts. One December afternoon he walked in after shoveling a heavy snowfall. His jacket was snow-covered and showed signs of a fabric rip. I inquired what had happened. He asked me to sit with him in the living room for a chat. That was the moment I knew we were in for an adventure not of our choosing. Jess had fallen while shoveling and hit the bumper. That explained the rip, but not the reason for the frequency of the events which up to this point he had not shared. He had seen our family physician a few weeks previous who heard a heart murmur, but dismissed any serious ramifications.

My nurse brain went on RED ALERT immediately. Through a lovely combination of Providence and the friendship of a family physician in another city, we were able to get an emergency cardiac consultation at the Royal Alex Hospital in Edmonton. The astonishing results of an early morning angiogram resulted in a call from the consulting doctor to my parent's home. I had driven back there to wait (a suggestion from the nursing staff). The tightness in his voice was more than evident over the phone. He told me to come immediately back to the hospital. I tried to be calm as I explained to my parents I needed to return probably to pick up Jess. I knew in my spirit that was not the case, but did not want my parents to be stressed out.

As I maneuvered our orange Mercury through snowy streets, I had a difficult time breathing. In, out, again-- in, out. What possibly went wrong? The result of that angiogram was a shock to the attending cardiologist. A tumor, squeezing the pulmonary valve almost shut, lay firmly lodged in his heart. Jess was scheduled for immediate open heart surgery at the University of Alberta Hospital.

Naturally this was a bomb in our Christmas activities, but somehow the family reunion went of without too many misses. Looking back at the exquisite timing (all members of Jess's family were due to be in Alberta, gathered from different parts of the world), we felt this unexpected interruption was divinely ordained and orchestrated. That assurance gave us courage and perspective during the coming years when much of the forthcoming news was discouraging.

The neoplasm was malignant—an overgrown clump of spindle-cell sarcoma—so rare no protocol for treatment was available at the time. Only 12 patients had been diagnosed with the condition and that came after autopsy! Over the course of the next 5 years additional open heart surgery as well as extensive thoracic surgery was necessary. We were told to "go home and live as though this had never happened". I want to keep this account free from excessive negativity, but that was foolish advice.

Lessons are to be learned from each life experience we are called upon to traverse. The post-op after care involved several different cancer specialists at the Cross Cancer Institute in Edmonton. One doctor assigned to us was arrogant and rude. His mannerisms left little room for kindling hope in the future. Perhaps he did not understand the values of Canadians. We left his examining room in silence. As we drove across the High Level Bridge enroute to home, Jess, who up to that time had not said a word, turned to me and asked quietly, *"Shall I stop the car and jump off now? Doesn't seem much else will help."*

Anger and hurt enmeshed themselves into a resolve to notify someone in authority at the Cross. Together we decided to wait for 6 weeks to allow our fury to cool before notifying the head of the Cross Institute, Dr. Anthony Fields. We crafted a letter, meticulous in details and verbatim quotes of the conversation we had with the previous doctor. Within 2 weeks we had a phone call from Dr. Fields himself stating he had transferred Jess' case to his own work load. Such a compassionate act was the beginning of recovery.

This step of standing up for ourselves was new to us. Meekness has always been a shining virtue to which most Christians aspire. No one admires a loudmouthed, ego-driven individual whose self-centerness contaminates the room air. There are times when appropriate action taken with a dose of kindness works for a better outcome. As I traveled around the province years later teaching stress management, I tried to empower participants to do what they had to do in order to correct perceived wrongs. In 3 different sessions, 3 different towns I had women come up after the session and ask if the name of the physician was Dr. So and So. All those families had been similarly crushed by this man's behaviour. I felt totally vindicated.

Another major learning experience for both of us was the stark fact we were sorely impoverished when it came to a support group. We determined to correct this void. The next time a crisis arose we had special people in place waiting and willing to help. Two years later, almost to the exact day, we found ourselves rushing to Edmonton where another open heart surgery was performed. The letdown after this episode was much more devastating than the initial event, mainly in part because we had not fully integrated the cancer experience into our own personal life inventory. We re-learned the lesson about life's fragility and the need to live each moment fully.

With the exception of specialized nuclear radiation in San Francisco (unavailable in Canada and paid for by Alberta Health),there seemed to be no reasonable treatment protocol. We accepted this. To embark on experimental chemotherapy was not a risk Jess was willing to take. He spent a few days at my parents lake cabin, alone and in prayer, wrestling with the future. A freak late May snowstorm was a challenge as he melted snow for water and heated the small venue with the ancient wood stove. For several days he was "marooned" on the premises by fallen trees and no electricity. When he returned from his private retreat, he set his face to finishing what he had been called to do and never looked back.

Jess had a dream which was a motivating factor for a number of years. The church had progressed/grown enough that a new sanctuary was a logical step. More than anything else, he wanted to oversee the project to its completion. On a warm spring Sunday in March, 1987, a sod turning ceremony was held. Everyone was in a celebratory mood. Little did they know we had been told by our medical overseer that the cancer had enveloped a large portion of his right lung. We made a decision to withhold that information until Monday when Jess called the board together for an early morning coffee and dropped the news. All stops were pulled out as the building committee dove into action. Volunteers were organized, work shifts posted, ladies provided meals---all in an effort to get a quality job done...in time!

A few days afterwards we drove down to the cabin at Sylvan Lake. Jess had constructed a tree house a few years previously. It had not weathered well after a lightening bolt mangled one of the supporting trees. We thought it prudent to dismantle it before anyone was injured due to its fragility. We spent the mild spring day chopping and burning. Close to sunset the job was finished. I was pushing snow on the ashes when a soft clanging sound caught my attention. Reaching down into the snow I saw an oval brooch which did not seem familiar. I brushed the debris from its whorls and held it out for my husband to see. He took a long moment before he mused *"Keep it. Someday it will have a message for you"*. What a strange declaration, I thought. Nonetheless, I washed and polished it once we were home then tucked it away at the bottom of my jewelry box. Months later as I began a grief walk of my own, I found it tucked away. Holding it in my hand, I pondered Jess' out-of the ordinary statement. What could this bauble teach me? The lesson? Even in the ashes of grief there is gold, if we take the time to find it. I have used that metaphor in every grief session I have taught since. One day mulling over old photographs, I came across a picture of Alice, the very same brooch fastened to the collar of a dressy blouse. I sat for a long time reflecting on the brooch and the story it unfolded.

We contacted Jess' parents, John and Edna Lynn, urging them to cut their term of mission service short and come home. They compiled and hopefully their colleagues in Kenya understood the dire nature of the decision. They returned to Alberta in July and spent the rest of the year living with us.

During the last 8 months of his life, Jess was granted a portion of grace and strength which allowed him to oversee the project to its completion. The contractor in charge, Robin Cruikshank, did a magnificent job of encouraging volunteers and subcontractors alike. All of us knew we were working against the forces of time. The dedication service was held on November 21, 1987. In spite of overwhelming fatigue and weakness, he chaired the dedicatory celebration. Severe pain caused him to leave the lunch early. Upon arriving home, he weakly smiled and said, *"I did it",* referring to the fact he had lived long enough to see his dream fulfilled.

His youngest sister Jillian graciously took a week long leave of absence to be with during this final crisis. She provided enormous "sisterly" support as we watched his light slowly dim.

Of interest is a brief vignette that happened just as I was assisting him getting dressed before the dedication service. Jess appeared to pass out—-became unresponsive and for a few minutes I thought he had died. Horrible thought, as it was my responsibility to get him to the service. My sister-in-law, Jillian, and I managed to tug his arms into his suit jacket and position him in a wheelchair. Out the door and into the car. All the time I am fervently praying under my breath, *"God, you can't let us down now!!! Help, help, help...."* We arrived at the church. A number of friends were standing by, waving encouragement. Jess allowed us to assist him out of the car, then straightened up, smiled and informed us, *"I don't need the wheelchair. I can walk in by myself!"* Which he did—triumphantly! I can only assume an invisible covering of strength and grace was his to enjoy for the next 2 hours.

We brought Regan home from his university studies at Trinity Western University. His request to have a leave of absence longer than a week was denied as the exam schedule was inflexible. The sting of that decision has not eased over the years. Renard and Rael were finishing their final year of high school. I had taken a 3 month leave of absence from my job at the Auxiliary Hospital.

Jess never left the house after the dedication service. Gradually the focus of his life narrowed. We had our closure chat. I knew what I had to do...buy a reliable car, arrange for 3 scholarships, and think about re-marrying. He told his sons his dreams for them. One memorable visit was from Pastor Glen Forsberg whom we had met during our time in Steinbach, Manitoba. Jess was too weak to engage in much conversation, but Glen just sat there by the bedside and was *present* with him. I was awed by his calm manner. On December 3, 1987, just before supper, his soul took flight. His parents along with the twins and myself eased him through the door to eternity by reciting the Lord's Prayer and singing *Great is Thy Faithfulness.*

My first act as a fresh widow was to tell my parents, who were downstairs in the living room, their beloved son-in-law was gone. Heartbroken, we sat together before I called our family doctor, Dr. Bryan Ward. He arranged for an ambulance to take the body to the hospital morgue. The on-call ambulance driver that evening was Garry Ezinga, a friend whom Jess had spent some time encouraging in various situations. At first I felt *"Oh no, not Garry..."* He asked if he could be alone with Jess for a few minutes. Of course. When he came downstairs, he was teary eyed and said *"I felt there were angels in that room".* Naturally this announcement helped ease the acute pain of the new loss.

A few days after the funeral a delegation from the church came to the house. They requested me to stay in Wainwright even though I had no "official" capacity as a clergywife. I did not tell them I had made that decision months earlier.

Six months before Jess' passing, I had mentally/emotionally relinquished my role as a pastor's wife. I knew in my heart he was to " be taken before his time", but did not feel released to say anything. I did not wish to be seen as uncaring, severely lacking in faith or abandoning the man I loved so much. In actuality, I was in the stage of anticipatory grief---something I would soon be teaching others. Doing "soul work" during those pre-sorrow months was a great benefit once I had entered the unfamiliar era of widowhood.

I moved through my loss recovery day by day. I was broken hearted, just did not have the appearance of one whose entire existence had been fractured. I mourned in the shower every morning. My Ford Taurus became a weeping chamber as I traveled back and forth to visit my parents, now in their nineties. Those were private venues where no one was party to the weeping. Not even my sons. From the wisdom granted by a distant vista, I now believe this was a primary error. Friends and acquaintances had no idea how much energy was expended dealing with grief. I must say I followed the lead of my mother-in-law who appeared stoic and did not give into tears readily. Two years later I summoned the courage to tell her I thought we had both been mistaken not to be "authentic" in our grief process. She agreed, and began to weep.

Part of my plan for managing the chaos following December3 was to remain active in the community, and if possible, become a bit more relaxed in my activities. I volunteered to work more Sundays in order to mitigate the pain of having to sit through the worship service as a former pastoral person.

In January 1988 I flew to Whitehorse, Yukon to visit Jillian. She resided in a cosy cabin on the south shore of Lake Labarge. The adjoining property sported a tiny, well-crafted Finnish sauna, heated by an ancient wood-stove. One frigid evening with a pristine star-show overhead, we indulged ourselves in a heated ritual followed by rolling naked (you read that correctly) in the newly fallen snow. How we laughed with the sheer joy of doing something bizarre. I kept thinking, *"What would my mother say if see saw me now?"* Then I thought *"Oh man, what if Jess can see me now. Maybe he can!!!"* Another round of giggles.

A few weeks after Jess died I wrote a column the local paper,*"The Wainwright Star-Chronicle".* It had been my pleasure to write a weekly column after a former contributor fell into disfavour for rather nasty commentaries on everything and everyone—including my husband! Readers began to complain about the vitriolic comments, threatening to pull their subscriptions if he was allowed to continue. A perfect opportunity for me to hone my writing skills! I promised the publisher I would produce a weekly column that would be entertaining and non-offending. He took me at my word and for 8 years I did exactly that. The column was entitled *"Lynnsight".*

The column as it appeared is as follows. Later that year, I won the Brimacombe Award which is given yearly to the author of the best column written for rural Alberta newspapers.

LIVING WHILE WATCHING YOUR DREAM DIE

Dreams sometimes die in the framework of uncertainty. Just because you cannot see the future does not mean there isn't one waiting for you.

If the bad things in life only happened to mean, irresponsible people, abusers of themselves and others, then the upright, kind and gentle folk could feel smug. But life doesn't happen that way. In the process of living, we are all maimed to a lesser or greater degree.

> *The head of a family who aspires to see his son harvest his land in the 21st century, may live to watch a dream that is 3 generations old smothered by bureaucracy and financial woes.*
>
> *What about a near-quarter of a century marriage, snatched away before the celebration of the silver anniversary by an uncontrollable disease?*
>
> *Every white-robed bride dreams her union will outlast all the aggravation to beat the odds of divorce. But one cannot amputate memories. They are there.*
>
> *Any parent who has observed a cherished child (whether in utero or beyond) lose the battle of life, knows what a dream feels like when it crushed.*
>
> *People are the authors and finishers of their own dreams to a large extent. The formation and fruition of a dream is a highly personal and deeply intricate exercise. Each individual has to take responsibility for his/her own goal. It is a "Task Impossible" for a spouse, children or siblings to do so. Even a mother cannot bring into being an adult child's dream. Ashes can be turned into building blocks if the call to be strong in the broken places is heeded. The perfect building material for a new dream is the dirt, tears and rubble of the smashed one. It takes creativity and a restored faith to accomplish such a task, but it can be done. Indeed, it MUST be done.*
>
> *A word for those who have been crushed watching their dreams shatter and the remnants turn to ashes. There are NEW dreams to be dreamed. Dreams that glow with the freshness of a new direction.*
>
> *Yes, you can surmount a broken dream and build a new one. Sure, it will take all the courage you can summon, but you must give it all you've got.*

One of the steps along the pathway of healing was the decision to have my ears pierced. In my original faith group, it wasn't exactly "kosher" for a pastor's spouse to desecrate (just jesting!) her ears with such contrivances. It seemed to me, however, the act would serve as a rite of passage in my new life. So one day in a bright and active mall in Penticton, B.C. I did the deed. Walked out of the shop with more courage than when I entered.

Prior to Jess's passing, I had been asked to assist a newly formed hospital committee whose responsibilities included the production of a history book to commemorate the Diamond Jubilee of the Wainwright and District Health Complex. I only consented because I believed it would prove to be an outlet for service once my days as a clergywife were finished. The chairman of the committee was Douglas White, a physician whose wife had died from a rare type of brain cancer 8 years previously.

A printer's deadline was looming for the history text. In order to expedite matters our dedicated group of fact-finders began meeting once a week. Several times the chairman, with his flair for hospitality, invited the entire group over for tea once the meeting had finished. Then one evening he invited just one member-me. Hmmmmmmmmmmmm.

A word of explanation. Douglas White was the most eligible widower around the area, He had endeared himself to everyone by being the perfect prototype of a family doctor. He truly was a beloved physician. Providence reigned a decade earlier in the choice of our family's medical care. We chose a young man who had recently moved to Wainwright and who later distinguished himself in the ranks of the Alberta Medical Association. Had Douglas been my physician of choice in 1978, this story would have come to a complete stop. It is considered highly unethical for doctors to develop romantic relationships with their patients!

I held him in high regard. In fact, the first time I addressed him as "Douglas" I nearly fainted from a combination of excitement and disbelief. On Valentine's Day I moved my wedding rings to my right hand. He noticed the switch, commenting on how well I looked!

We courted (dating seemed an inappropriate term considering our age/stage!) in clandestine fashion for many months before appearing together at a public function in Wainwright that autumn. I was prepared to limit our relationship to the uh—-platonic type. It seemed a bit preposterous from a variety of angles. I felt the searing stares from a couple of available widows who had been hoping for years to catch his fancy. His children, according to my recollection, had another lady in mind for his affections.

As mature adults (Douglas was 19 years my senior), we took a l-o-n-g look at what happening to both of our hearts. I had awakened feelings in him which had long been buried and in his typical Scottish demeanor, he was not about to jump into a permanent relationship just because HE WAS MADLY IN LOVE! Oh no—we dissected the meaning of love as opposed to infatuation for weeks , maybe months, on end. As time progressed we "broke up" on 3 different occasions. One time, after a tearful farewell driving home from a theater production in Edmonton, I marched into several heavy duty evening shifts at work. No one was aware of the prevailing ache in my spirit.

After the last shift I arrived home around midnight to find a neat bundle on the staircase. Douglas had dropped off a gift for my birthday. Enclosed in the packaging was a brochure for an upcoming family medicine convention in Banff. A handwritten scribble on the card asked, *"would you like to come with me?"* The gift? The most gorgeous silk camisole and half-slip from Holt Renfrew. Now then, what kind of mixed message was THAT???? We had a chat the very next morning.

Douglas introduced me to a new world of thinking. He was raised Presbyterian, attended the local United Church and professed a strong faith. He loved the Bible, and had the same value system as mine, but expressed it with different vocabulary. Attending the worship services at the United Church with him was an interesting enterprise. Picture the quizzical looks. In a comic sort of was it was *"What's up, Doc?"* I credit the times I spent in services very different from my accustomed habits, to the opening of my heart to the beauty of liturgy. The appreciation of ritual ceremony has never faded over the years.

I suspected our relationship was on the path to matrimony when he declared one day while visiting my cabin at Sylvan Lake, *"What we need here is a microwave oven!"* I quickly countered,*"Excuse me, we certainly DO NOT need one. This place is lovely and primitive just as it is!"* Four months later he had the nerve to buy and install one sans my permission. I was doomed!!

His duties as a member of a provincial medical committee entailed a fair amount of travel. We joined a group of dedicated citizens who met to promote the need for palliative care in our area. We were asked to fly to Victoria to tour the Palliative Care Unit in a hospital there. It was a fun trip, but I could not shed the guilt-inducing thought, *"What will people think?"* I spent a good deal of time praying to be invisible! We spent a couple of hours at Butchard Gardens. We were nearing a gorgeous display of roses when our reverie was interrupted by a shrieky cry, *"Oh Dr. White, so good to see you. And who is this?"* looking at me with eagle eyes. Turned out it was a former patient (insert busy body) from years ago. Well, we knew the whole town would soon know of our "fact finding" trip.

When we traveled together we always booked 2 rooms. I kept the receipts as a salvo for my need to justify any actions which seemed improper to those bent on criticizing. My cousin Norma once chuckled, *"Virginia, just because you pay for 2 rooms doesn't mean you use them!"* Is that not a tantalizing thought?

Early in 1990 we decided to marry. Before we sealed our engagement with a ring, Douglas formally asked my parents for their blessing. My father started to cry, and said *"Oh, I am so happy she won't be a widow any longer".* As we left their apartment Douglas turned to me and asked if I had understood what Norman had said. Naturally I thought I would be a wife again for a long, long time.

We decided on a ring that was symbolic of our union. I put it away until all of our children had been informed. A day later, Douglas called to inform me one of his colleagues had phoned to congratulate him on our engagement! Who saw us at the jewelry store? We will never know.

The world during the late 1980s and early 1990s was in a pretty good space. The generation, now known as the Millennials, were crying their way into birthing rooms, rumours of Nelson Mandela's soon release from prison and the end of apartheid in South Africa were widespread. Robert Fulghum's *"All I Really Need to Know I Learned in Kindergarten"* was a best seller.

My personal world was bright and beautiful also. I gave my "swan song' sermon to the congregation 6 months after Jess's passing, encouraging all of us to step bravely into a new adventure with a new leader. The church board very wisely waited for the members to properly mourn before hiring another pastor. The assembly had grown; it was vigorous enough to call another young man to be an associate alongside the lead pastor. A small elegant wedding was planned for May. Looking forward to a new chapter in life, my worries were few.

One unseasonably warm January Sunday I walked to church. I knew my friends would be there to congratulate me on my engagement news. I noticed Rev. Marvin Dynna from our denomination's provincial headquarters in Edmonton was in the audience, but thought nothing of it. At the close of the sermon and just before the benediction, the lights were dimmed and Rev. Dynna reached into his jacket pocket. He began to read a letter which informed all of us present that the pastor had been involved in a moral failure. He had immediately resigned. A more accurate term would have been "run away".

From mile high joy to ground zero horror in less time than it took to draw a breath. Stunned to the core, most of us began to softly weep. No one wanted to know the details. I was playing the organ that morning. I managed to keep upright and play with closed eyes. Feeling too wrung out to walk home, I called Douglas for a ride. We sat in silence for a long time, trying to fathom the repercussions of this affair. The effects were almost immediate. A domino-like situation followed. This was around the time of the "Jimmies" scandal (Swaggart and Bakker). People just lost faith in the integrity of ministers and chose not to align themselves with any organized church. Heart-breaking and maddening all at the same time. The associate, Rev. Derek Hamre, took over the reins as the church limped into some sort of recovery.

Meanwhile, the 2 families that were about to become blended accustomed themselves to a new beginning which would affect them in various ways. We set the date for early May, determined to keep the wedding celebration a quiet, closed event. I was scheduled to work an evening shift prior to the wedding day. I figured it was just too close for comfort, so arranged with a very good friend , Helen Schmidt, to replace me without giving notice to our supervisor, Mary Pilson. Naturally there was a bit of breath indrawing when Helen showed up without an adequate explanation of "why". On May 5, 1990 a mutual friend, Dr. David Skelton, married us in Edmonton's All Saints Cathedral. His combined career as a gerontologist and Anglican clergyman made him the perfect officiant.

The transition into the "White House" was ...fun. I rented out my home on 2nd Avenue to a local minister's family as I began the transition to a new life chapter. Douglas' late wife, Maureen, was an amazing lady. Classical pianist, artist, gold-metal horticulturist, I could go on! I didn't know the difference between a perennial and a seedling. Don't tell me the Almighty has no sense of humour! I learned the ins and outs of gardening faster than you can say, "These Veronica plants need transplanting to a sunnier place".

Being a physician's wife had many similarities to that of a clergywife. For example, appearance is VERY important. Never appear in public as though you just fell out of bed. Do not cling to your husband as if he were the last board on a sinking raft. Do not do anything outrageous which might bring embarrassment to your partner. Never, NEVER break confidentiality. And so forth!

We decided it would be wise for me to take a yearlong leave of absence from nursing to become properly adjusted in my new role as Douglas' wife. This move had to be approved by the hospital's administration. Actually , the decision had a long history reaching back into Hebrew scriptures that advised newly weds to have a year's break from regular duties!

What a year it was! Within the space of several months we celebrated the 30th anniversary of my nursing class in Toronto, as well as traveling to Edinburgh, Scotland to attend the 40th year reunion of his medical class. It was a gathering of doctors from every corner of the world. A number of his classmates had become well-known for their expertise in their field of interest. I was asked to present a "small something" on what it was like to be a (relatively) new bride married to a dyed-in-the-wool Scotsman. A number of erudite presentations were also scheduled. Topics ranged from the intricacies of practicing medicine in the South Pacific to the molecular components of diverse chemicals. And then there was mine! The speech was well received amid howls of laughter. I refused to let my husband pre-read the text, so he had no idea what was coming. Douglas later stated I had made him famous, a wonderful compliment. The following is more (or less) what I said.

****

CANADIAN WIFE TELLS ALL!! WELL, NOT QUITE--

You are probably quite unaware that I am the only one here this evening who is being paid a fee to do this. Douglas is paying me handsomely NOT to tell all!

Love and romance are indiscriminate. They cross all barriers. I think you will agree. How is it possible for a woman with an Irish background to fall madly in love with someone who is absolutely, undeniably Scottish? There have been many occasions this past year when I have asked, "Why me, Lord?" The answer is always the same, "Why not you?"

DSW is the epitome of all you expect in a true gentleman. I incorrectly assumed all his forefathers woud be like-minded. Other brides read books like "The Ideal Marriage" or "The Joy of Cooking". Not me. I began devouring articles on Scottish history. I cannot tell you how horrified I was when I read the bloody exploits of the Campbells and the MacDonalds.

One terrible evening in front of a glowing fireplace I read the Oxford Book of Political Anecdotes. After trying to assimilate the accounts of

James 1 and several awful beheadings, I had to take an aspirin to help me sleep. And you must know that is against my religious convictions.

When I discovered my beloved belonged to the MacGregor clan, my dismay rose to astronomical proportions. I was born and raised in cattle country, Alberta, Canada. People are wonderfully rewarded with money if they are instrumental in rounding up cattle rustlers. Lo and behold, I had agreed to marry one! What was I going to tell my mother?

Right from the beginning we have had friendly arguments on pronunciation. Who is to be the judge here? When I feel as though I may be losing the argument, I always remark smugly, 'Its a poor man who can't find two ways to pronounce a word". I'm quoting somebody famous, but I can't remember exactly whom.

In the Canadian Rockies there is a very famous sightseeing spot called Craigalechie. How did I know it had a connection to his homeland? For years I pronounced it differently. No one seemed to notice or even care, for that matter. I was informed early on in our courtship the politically correct pronounciation. Oh, well......

As with all newlyweds, we discovered we had a few irreconcilable differences. Alas, this was after the wedding ceremony so we had to come to terms with them. I used to think there was no life before coffee in the morning. Douglas soon confessed to me the smell of coffee made him feel nauseous. He was bigger than me so I knew I had to change my priorities. I switched from drinking coffee in the morning to sipping tea. Of course, the fact it was served to me in bed sweetened the adjustment considerably. In addition, I have always slept with a window open. Good for the constitution, referring to one's physiology, naturally. Not so with my new groom. We negotiated a compromise. The window is open Monday, Wednesday and Friday, closed on Tuesday, Thursday and Saturday. Sunday is the choice of the last one to bed.

Another thing. I believe in vitamins, and Douglas doesn't. Shocking, isn't it? However, he gets a lot of samples through the mail, and I feel compelled to eat them so they won't be wasted. It is enough to shake his value system.

Guess what I love in ascending order? Freshly squeezed lemon juice on vegetables, walking quickly and neat tabletops. Guess what he dislikes in ascending order. You know already, don't you?

Within 4 months of our wedding date, I became a surrogate grandmother, twice over. It has been a wonderful experience, but I still think Douglas was a bit sneaky about things. He proposed to me, and THEN informed me of the babies anticipated arrival. Not cricket was it? Then again, sleeping with a grandfather is pretty heady stuff.

He worried about his sons setting up viable family practices while I laid awake at night wondering if my sons would find employment after graduating from university. Blending a family of 11 adults and 2 babies is a fascinating process.

We have vastly different styles of driving. Actually my style of driving is a sensitive area with me. I have never had an accident, altho' the good Lord knows how many I've caused. I do not know if Douglas has ever had a citation for speeding—ah, would he even admit that?-- but I have. Only three, I can swear to that. Any car I have ever owned always carries this unwritten law invisibly taped to the windshield. If a person feels free to backseat drive, I feel free to tell them to get out and walk. Works wonders because it tends to halt irretractable nagging. I have never had to enforce it, but there is always the first time.

Marrying Douglas White has proved to be better than an antibiotic, more effective than a steroid and infinitely more fun than psychoanalysis. In short, it was one of the smartest things I have ever done.

****

A decision was made in 1991 to demolish the summer cabin my father had built on the north shore of Sylvan Lake. It seemed sensible to have a more permanent dwelling to accommodate the blended family. We designed it according to our needs restricted by a budget. The house Jess and I bought when we first arrived in Wainwright sold for a fair market price. We organized the plans around that amount. A moderate sized loan was all that was necessary to buy the appliances and basic furniture. Thinking ahead to the possibility of an "arthritic retirement" the layout was considered one in which we could age in place. Our plan was to remain in Wainwright until the year 2000, take a well-planned trip to some exotic place and move down to Sylvan after I retired from nursing. The act of dreaming dreams keeps one vital and alive!

To accommodate the sentimentality attached to the humble cabin in which I had spent most of my childhood summers, we saved the doors, cedar siding , the antique furniture among other items. I promised my parents I would incorporate them into the finished décor of the house. In a contemplative way, it was a metaphor depicting the new beginning using older familiar parts to further my story.

Shortly after our wedding, I made the choice to throw my hat (or was it my head?) into the ring, so to speak, in an attempt to win the Reform candidacy for the federal constituency of Vegreville. Canadian politics was in a lather with a not-so quiet revolt in the Western provinces. This foray into politics took courage and a whole lot of other attributes! I was pitted against 3 men as we toured the area, each one of us stating our commitment to the party platform and explaining why we were passionate about making a difference in our country. In case anyone still wonders, politics is a blood sport. I rather suspect every political organization has a similar grid that extracts a toll from anyone brave enough to venture down that path.

Douglas was my biggest supporter. We practiced speeches together. Often he would play the role of an audience adversary on divisive topics like family values, farm subsidies and global trade views. In June of '92, after an excellent campaign, the nomination meeting was held. I was not the successful candidate, but left the building with my head held high knowing I had "fought fairly and valiantly". During the entire process I felt I had been enriched (not MONETARILY!) in ways that forfeit vocabulary. It is worth noting the successful candidate, Mr. Leon Benoit, went on to win the seat in the next federal election a year later. He invited me to open his campaign office with a blessing a few weeks later. It was my pleasure to do so.

We had a cup of tea at home once the evening was behind us. Douglas remarked wistfully, *"There must be a reason why you didn't win."* I agreed, noting that in time we would know the answer. We had to wait until the following summer.

The ensuing months were busy. We traveled to California, enjoyed the gorgeous vistas of B.C. and found time to write a play which was produced by the local theater company. I sat on the board of the local Credit Union and learned another side of life.

In January of '93 I was asked to present a session on "Coping with Change" to a group of ministers meeting for an annual conference. I did my best to convince them change provided an opportunity for growth, even though it was viewed at times as an adversary to be fought. It proved to be a current subject. VERY current as a matter of fact. Lunch and fellowship followed the presentation. I decided to stop in at the lake house before heading back to Wainwright. The phone was ringing as I pushed open the front door. It was Douglas. I heard him gasp weakly, *"I'm having a heart attack, ambulance on the way".* The phone sounded as if it had been dropped, and then died. Frantic, I phoned the ER at the Wainwright Hospital to be sure I had heard correctly. A quick call to C.P Blakely School in Sylvan Lake where Regan was beginning his student teacher practicum. I knew I could not safely drive home in a distressed state. With Regan at the wheel we made it to Wainwright in record time—just as the ambulance was pulling out with its precious cargo bound for the University Hospital in Edmonton. I was granted time to plant a kiss on his cheek before the siren and lights indicated an emergency trip was underway.

The cardiac event was severe enough to destroy all but a fifth of his heart's capacity. Naturally many planned activities were placed on the "later or never" shelf. We postponed a trip to France until the following spring, fully expecting a return to some kind of normalcy. The early summer months revolved around cardiac rehabilitation. By July we thought we were out of the woods. A trip to Whitecourt to visit Rael and Leanne included a hike along the shore of the Athabasca River gathering river stones to place in our "yarden" at Sylvan. We took an art course together (total waste of time and money!).

The world at large was relatively stable in August 1993. Buckingham Palace opened its doors to the public for the first time, Ben Johnson was banned from athletics for life and the late Robin Williams was his funniest best in the movie *"Mrs. Doubtfire"*. My partner's health was beginning to be perilous but I was blissfully unaware.

I drove to Sylvan Lake one day to check out a few things at the house. That evening he phoned. Intuitively I knew something was awry. In measured terms he told me he had diagnosed himself a few days previous—a tumor in his lower bowel.

He didn't know how to break the ghastly news to me, but could I meet him in Edmonton the next morning for a doctor's appointment? Stunned beyond words I placed the phone back in its cradle and tried to assimilate the meaning of the message. All I could think of was *"fresh hell."* Foreseeing the near future in a flash I walked through the entire house lamenting with bitter gut cries.

X-rays and barium studies proved the dire self-diagnosis to be correct. The next hurdle was informing our families, which the "doctor in the house' was extremely reluctant to do. I worked a couple of shifts all the while hiding this enormous secret which threatened to spill over every moment. I finally called a good friend who lived out of town, also a registered nurse, and blurted out my situation. Irene Clarence consoled me with prayer and sealed lips.

Eventually due to the nature of the tumor, Douglas began to endure bowel obstruction and emergency surgery was necessary. The surgeon, Dr. Warwick, called me at 5 a.m. to inform me Douglas had done well during the operation, but regrettably the tumor was at Stage 1V, meaning it had invaded much of the abdominal cavity. He offered gentle sympathy. I quieted myself and rushed to the University Hospital. As I greeted him trying to be brave , he said sorrowfully, *"Its such disappointing news, isn't it?"*

The designation Stage 1V meant the likelihood of a cure was

remote. In other words, his days were most definitely numbered. No chemotherapy or radiation was even suggested because of the apparent terminal condition. All we had was our love---and very little time. I was grief-stricken with the thought of a repeat widowhood.

Douglas had been told "alternative facts" about his early childhood in Scotland. A half-brother he did not know existed had contacted him a few years earlier. It took time and a measure of grace to rearrange his thought patterns about his original family. The previously planned trip to France was to be a journey to settle some long standing questions. It seemed now that the opportunity to do so had slipped away. Voicing our down-heartedness to his surgeon, Dr. Warwick looked at me with a steadfastness that gave me courage and said, *"Virginia, you can do this. I will write a letter for the airlines, give you a prescription for morphine. Help your husband finish up this life business".*

Great---except neither of us were bilingual. The perfect solution was his daughter Sheila who spoke French. A fairly good post-op period followed, but liver involvement proved to be distressing. We were able to have a consult with Dr. Fields at the Cross Cancer institute who arranged for several emergency radiation treatments to shrink the liver and alleviate some of the pain. It worked! With a cache of analgesia, letters from the doctor and a huge bundle of grit we flew to France in mid-October.

Our 10 days there were flawless, except of course, Douglas was dying by degrees. The pictures we took of the new family connections betray none of his deteriorating condition. Somehow we were given the grace and strength to accomplish what had to be done. We flew home after a scary crisis, arriving home on Election Day 1993. We watched the results on TV as the Conservatives were decimated across the country while the Reformers galloped onto the national stage with breathtaking savvy.

Douglas turned to me and remarked, eyes filled with tears, *"If things had been different, your would have been a member of Parliament now."* I softly reminded him that winning was unimportant now that I was losing him. Here in bold relief was the reason I did not win the nomination to run for the Reform Party. Fresh grief and the vigorous adjustment to Ottawa did not seem to be a harmonious combination.

Days flowed into nights. I called his children and asked them to come as soon as possible. I knew the signs of a life closing in on itself. Six days after arriving home, just before the sun rose on All Saints Eve, and surrounded by the people who loved him most, Douglas' soul took flight.

The descent into this second widowhood precipitated a fresh set of questions and triggered a troupe of ragged emotions. I thought I had learned in meticulous detail the necessary lessons in life the first time around. Apparently not. My involvement in CanSurmount, a nation-wide support group for those affected by cancer, was a direct result of Jess' diagnosis. Seminars on bereavement and loss recovery were now a part of a growing portfolio. Blending 2 families had been realized with relative success. I figured after 1990 all my Christmases would be *White*. An entire bundle of plans we had so carefully devised, cities we wanted to see together---the remnants now lay at my doorstep with daunting irretrievably.

As a visible symbol to everyone who came to visit, but mostly for myself, I fashioned an elegant black velvet bow and tacked it to the outside door frame. It hung there for 40 days. At the end of that period, I took it down and celebrated the fact I had survived with a cup of tea and a piece of fruitcake. This too shall pass, I reminded myself.

I once read 2 statements which suddenly became part of my emotional vestments.

> *Everything you experience in life moulds you as a person. The more you experience, the more you understand.* ANON
> *"Meaning" makes a great many things endurable, perhaps everything."* CARL JUNG

One quiet evening I sat at the oak table in the small room overlooking the south patch of the garden. The specimen trees were barren, but I knew the roots were working feverishly waiting for the spring sun to beckon them into verdant life again. I scribbled this poem on a piece of scrap paper before tucking it away in my journal.

>FROM THE PORTAL OF GRIEF
>Two loves
>Two lives
>Two losses
>Third life.
>Two streams
>   join
>One river
>   divided
>One stream
>Finding her own way.
>Why again??
>Recurrent question.
>Why not again?
>Recurrent answer.
>You enriched me so much.
>Death took away so much.
>But I am not poverty-stricken.

A wise painter knows that every aspect of the underpainting has a purpose. Grisaille is a term designating an underpainting in shades mostly of gray. This was the dominate feeling I endured during the few months following Douglas' passing. Hand-ground colours mixed with a drop or two of rich oils are useful for an easy spread. Shadows are often stroked in at this stage. It is important for the painting to be set aside now in order for it to become thoroughly dry. Further work can proceed once a semi-matte finish is apparent.

A Career-Wise Shift

A FEW SHORT hours after Douglas' passing I sat on the living room sofa and reflected on my life, past, present and future. I was supremely aware that requisite changes were about to be made. I needed Divine wisdom. The possibility of running pell-mell into the future with an unhealed spirit always awaits the broken hearted. I determined not to fall into that pit. Quietly a three-point plan took shape. It became a beacon that never dimmed as I moved my way into a new normal. Three prospects figured in the equation. I just needed to work out the details to enhance each one. No problem!

I decided I would embark on a career of chaplaincy, resign/retire from nursing on November 30, 1994 and move down to the lake house by Christmas. In less than an hour, the skeleton (?sketch, perhaps in light of this theme) of my future had taken shape. No one was privy to these plans. After all, in my sessions on grief recovery I was always firm in denouncing rapidly made plans that involved moving or severe switching of jobs. I didn't want to appear hypocritical so I quietly made plans without public notification.

Slowly I adjusted to "skin hunger", the longing to be held and lovingly touched. I dreaded coming home to a darkened house after evening shifts at the hospital. Sometimes I would sit for several moments summoning up the pluck needed to enter the house with its insufferable quietness.

Someone once wrote (spare me, the name of the author escapes me, but in order to have it in print, they must be famous!) , *"Anxiety arises out of having too many options."* I have a different perspective. Listing my options gave me a sense of harmony that assured me I had the ability to make excellent decisions. An undated journal entry shortly after the funeral follows.

WHAT ARE MY OPTIONS?
1. Continue part-time at the Auxiliary,
2. Go full time at the Auxiliary.
3. Continue free-lancing part time.
4. Full time free-lancing.
5. Train as a chaplain.
6. Become a consultant on "Dying at Home".
7. Stay in Wainwright.
8. Move to Sylvan Lake.
9. Remain single (THIS DOES NOT PRECLUDE THE OCCASIONAL WARM EXCELLENT RELATIONSHIP!)
10. Volunteer more.
11. Travel more.
12. Get back into politics.

For a while I experienced what is known as "cognitive dissonance". My circumstances had changed but my essential self had not. The two were no longer a tidy "fit". I needed a time frame to "dry out", in the language of a master painter. A space to catch my breath , steady my equilibrium and be at peace with my reality. The initial months of 1994 allowed me that endowment.

My mind began the task of seriously exploring my planned career shift. Soon the idea grew into a workable plan. Details were an obvious lack, but my life as I knew it was due for an alteration. I was about to "reinvent" myself. Actually, Douglas had used that phrase a couple of years previously when I was expanding my horizons. John Sartre once remarked, *"A person can improve their autobiography".* I was about to start on mine!

My two careers (nursing and theology) were a perfect combination for an interesting future. Chaplaincy seemed to connect them in a congruent tandem. My cards were very close to my heart as I submitted preliminary information to the supervisor of the Clinical Pastoral Education at the Royal Alexandra Hospital in Edmonton. The subsequent interview went well, except Dr. Costain kept probing about my sense of abandonment by God. Other emotions may have surfaced, but Divine abandonment wasn't among them. Several weeks skipped by before I had the letter in my hand which assured I was accepted into the extended program due to commence in September.

Around this same time another cloud of sorrow was beginning to form and descend. Both my parents had become noticeably more fragile. Dad was in hospital recovering from an overblown infection, but anticipating a discharge order a few days hence. His physician promised him if he could walk around the ward 3 times without stopping, he could go home. He diligently practiced the routine every day.

One morning I had an appointment with a lawyer in Vermilion to sign a document which said in essence I accepted the terms of Douglas's will. Of course I had no intention of grieving anything written therein, but certain legalities had to be followed. I drove home and prepared to work an evening shift. Within moments of my arrival home, an R.C.M.P. Officer was at the door, his hat held respectfully over his heart. Instantly I knew "bad news". Mom had toppled over in the wee hours of March 1. It pained me to know she had died alone. Norma had phoned the Auxiliary when she could not reach me by phone. The manager canceled my shift and phoned the police to keep an eye out for me.

When the news was gently broken to me, my first expectation was that my father would expire of a broken heart. Their 67th anniversary was on the threshold. Nevertheless, his spunky Irish spirit pulled him through the first ravages of mourning. He told me where his good

Sunday suit was hanging in the closet and could I please bring it for him to wear to the funeral. He stopped walking, however. Never took another step from that day forward. I suppose it was his way of reconciling his loss.

Long-term care facilities were overflowing and all had a waiting list in 1994. Not much has changed in the ensuing decades! Arranging placement for my father was an experience fortified with a few miracles and embellished with bated breath. A few times I thought the word nightmare would have been more descriptive. Watching him adjust valiantly to the new routine with all the limitations further fractured my heart.

One of the agonizing aspects of advanced elderhood is the ghastly reality of loneliness. Having celebrated 98 birthdays, most of my father's friends were either deceased, demented or disabled. He was initially placed in a room with another elderly gentleman. The room was divided by a hand drawn curtain. The prospect of having a roommate did not engender kind feelings in the original occupant. We drew the curtain closed and helped dad arrange his things in his new setting. My sons and I left for a few minutes to speak to the supervisor. No sooner had we left than the other resident poked his head through the curtain opening and yelled at dad to *"Get out of here!"* When we returned my father was in tears. He was convinced he had experienced a hallucination and was on the verge of a mental breakdown. Regan promptly went over to the offender, bent close to his ear and said,*"If you ever do anything to my Grampa there will be BIG TROUBLE!"* As the world turns, he passed away from a stroke 2 weeks later!

The impact of all the layered losses vouchsafed a levy on my emotional status. I escaped for a few day to the house at Sylvan Lake. Its quietude facilitated reflection and promoted further decision making. Bidden or not, God was present. When I allowed myself to be attentive, I felt the nudging of the Divine. It strengthened my resolve to resign my nursing career and move to Sylvan Lake, even though I had no idea how I was to earn a livelihood. A test of faith was on the horizon.

The months motored on. The "White House" was placed on the market. I wrote out my official resignation and proceeded to carry out one of my late husband's wishes. We had originally planned a trip to Ireland to finish off the odyssey to France. However a worsening of Douglas' condition during the final days in France precluded those plans. Air Canada kindly refunded the fare of that leg of the trip once we explained the circumstances. During our closure chat, he indicated he wanted me to take the trip to Ireland as we had planned. In addition, holding my hand, *"I want you to marry again."* Oh no. PLEASE DO NOT SAY THAT! I kept silent on the last request, but nodded an affirmative half-smile for the trip.

The trip to Dublin and beyond was booked for September. It began as a basic search for Norman's Celtic roots. However, a phone call from Florida followed by a late summer visit by a gentleman called Kenneth changed the itinerary into a multi-faceted reflection on Divine sovereignty and providence. More about that aspect in another chapter.

The Clinical Pastoral Education sessions began in October under the excellent tutorship of Rev. Dr. Neil Elford. The group of 6 eager wannabe chaplains had been garnered from 12 applicants. We were a *very* diverse cluster from various faith backgrounds and assorted life experiences. This melange was deliberate. What was the use of spending time with folks whose thought patterns correlated with one's own? No learning advancement there—just smiling and a sense of agreement. Over the course of 7 months we sparred and argued with one another, often groaning in dismay at the actions of one member in particular. Each of us pushed our own individual "sacred cows'" as far as we dared. I moved out of my comfort zone and instead, embraced possibility.

We were required to keep a log of all the patients we had the privilege to encounter. How did our feelings respond when we had to answer tough questions? Did we feel at ease with those who did not share our particular value system? How did we show the love of God to Muslims, atheists, First Nations members?

I had so much to learn! Along the way I made more than a few embarrassing mistakes. One time I was called to minister to a young couple whose baby had died before she had been given a chance to live. They asked me to baptize the infant. Coming from a faith background different than mine I supposed this was a way of comforting them. I prepared a tender ceremony and proceeded to pray with them. Oh oh---not a wise choice. Rev. Elford called me into his office as soon as he read my report and gently admonished me about the purpose of baptism. A naming ceremony would have been a better choice. I was duly mortified and repentant. The incident was mentally filed under the category "zeal without knowledge".

Re-reading the learning covenant which I drew up at the onset of the C.P.E. basic unit affirms an inner conviction I have indeed come a long way. A summary of the covenant follows.

NEED	OBJECTIVE
To stop feeling I have to justify everything I do	To explore underlying reasons about this
A rekindling of my ardor for active ministry	To experience a "kick start" encounter
Completion of my own grief work	Confront memories of sad events
Reduce my fear and ignorance of AIDS	Seize opportunities to work with AIDS patients
Reduce any layers of bias which prevent true compassion	Recognize and take aim at prejudices
Increase my knowledge of native culture, especially healing arts	Seek out opportunity to work with First Nations members
A sense of equipoise in E.R. situations with strangers	Work enough shifts to develop confidence

At the completion of our unit, I wrote this about the relationship to the supervisor, Rev. Elford.

A feeling of trust, built over months of encounters, is an entity not to be taken lightly. Right from the beginning of this course I felt anything I told Neil behind those closed doors of his office would NEVER leave there. That is a great motivator to be honest. I felt you were absolutely and completely honourable in the area of confidentiality.

I remember the day in February when you told me I was coy and seductive during our times of supervision. (This presumably in an effort to have you say the things you thought I wanted to hear.) Then you did a little imitation of my body language. I must say it was SEVERELY lacking in finesse, but nonetheless... You went on to remark you were not going to give me what I wanted. (Dear Father Above, YOU know my heart was pure in thought!!). But in fact, you did exactly that. I wanted to learn to acknowledge the areas of glaring weakness, crippling limitations and so on. You helped me do precisely that. The process is not over, but what a shove you gave me. You helped me understand it can be quite affirming to feel useless at times.

One of the greatest gifts you gave me was the ability to recognize and identify my internal critic. Not until this past month have I clued into "theological reflection" I can only imagine with a sense of disquiet how much my struggles must have grated you.

The foregoing became part of my final evaluation which remains on permanent record.

During that initial unit of Clinical Pastoral Education (plus 2 others which followed in succeeding years) I learned a number of things about myself, which had remained covered with various euphemisms. First of all, I was in the category of "rescuer". If I could not help to resolve another's problem, it affected me on a deep level. I needed to know I was capable of coming to someone's aid and fixing it. I suppose I always knew that propensity at a subconscious level, but now I had the vocabulary to express it. Secondly, I was "over sensitive". I heard the exhortation to do better, but often missed the affirmation and invitation to do so. Big difference there. In supervisory sessions I was frequently confronted with my need to justify everything I did. I learned to check out my assumptions and repeat often in exasperating situations," *Whose event is this anyway?"*

I had to trust God to provide the best possible "mix" of colleagues in all the C.P.E. modules. In each one of the three, there were individuals who positively grated me beyond belief. I figured that was okay because I knew they felt the same way about me! The last 2 modules were taken at the Tampa General Hospital in Tampa, Florida. It is designated as a "not for profit" facility. The supervisor was Rev. Dr. Dan McRight whose approach in teaching his students was entirely different from what I had previously enjoyed. That said, it was a tremendous experience of growth. Both times I was the only Canadian and as well as the only person of charismatic persuasion. In addition the last group consisted of 4 young men, and me! Three of the gentlemen had left their respective vows behind, forsook the mother church and had married. That provided a good amount of interesting discussion. I inquired if I could take extra assignments and duties in order to achieve "advanced status". Armed with an affirmative answer I worked extra hard to be granted this designation.

My colleagues in these sessions were the facilitators who forced me to take a severe inward look at some of my basic assumptions. I will always be grateful for those (sometimes unpleasant) encounters. I also learned to confront male authority figures without breaking out in a rash, or worse, weeping.

One of the requirements was the writing in detail of our encounters, good or poor, with the patients on our assigned units. We were encouraged to ask ourselves, *"How am I like this woman?" "How am I NOT like her?" "Can I discern this patient's greatest need?"*

A Career-Wise Shift

"What would be the most helpful thing I can offer"? "What gift does she unconsciously give me?" The following is an actual account of one such pastoral visit.

> Mrs. Y. is a 64 year old lady whose age-worn face has a lot of stories to tell. On June 3, an electrical explosion in her trailer home ignited an afghan covering her. The resulting fire totally destroyed her home, leaving her right arm and entire chest ravaged with burns. It was estimated 10% of her body was burned. During her hospitalization she was part of a research project to study the absorption rate of a new drug. This was a joint effort of TGH's burn unit and the University of South Florida.
>
> For some unexplainable reason she lost the motivation to eat. Her decreased appetite became a primary concern. Mrs. Y. began to exhibit "odd behavior" and a consult was sent to a Dr. Powers (neuro or pysch—I know not which!!) This bit of information piqued my interest a lot. However, the doctor's handwriting was so abominably humbo-jumbo I could not decipher what the odd behavior entailed.
>
> I had just settled in nicely when an RN came into our space and apologetically announced she need a laxative...and it wasn't of the oral variety. Out I went dutifully, promising I would be back in a wee while. In my haste to leave, I absentmindedly left my purse on her bedside table. Upon arriving at the nursing station, I was reduced to a lather because I couldn't remember where I had left it. I returned 15 minutes later and once again settled in. No sooner had I arranged my body and soul in a straight line when the patient suddenly sat straight up and loudly said "she had to go"...and she didn't mean out on a date! The wild look in her eye caused me to leap up instantly to find a nurse who could be of more assistance than myself at that moment. Once again I left for a while. When I came back the deed was done---I could tell by the atmospheric conditions!

> *In my determination to GET THIS DERN INTERVIEW DONE, I plopped right down on the bedpan which had been carefully placed on the chair. I hasten to add it was covered with a towel, but still....Thank God it was empty. As you can imagine I was not feeling the least bit useful or charitable. She did not appear to notice or care.*

A number of exiled Cubans were patients during my time there. One elderly man had interesting stories to tell of deprivation under the Castro regime. I affirmed his bravery in fleeing the rigors and tears of leaving many of his family members. He patted my hand and said, "*Well, you remind me of an iron petunia.*" My puzzled look must have given him pause as he explained, "*You know, that movie of the women who stood up against the men...*" The light dawned. "*You mean the movie Steel Magnolias?* " I loved that designation and often think of myself in those terms!

During my first unit of C.P.E. I renewed my ministerial credentials with my original faith group. I had voluntarily given them up when I married Douglas. At the time it seemed my life was heading in another direction. I would not be engaged in active ministry again, certainly not of the parish type. There was an unexplainable delay in the granting of them. In the meantime I entered a barren place spiritually. I questioned every facet of faith, and was open in discussing my disillusionment with the hierarchy that seemed to have so many irrelevant issues. For a short time I even considered joining the Quakers. The fact there was no nearby meeting house was a hindrance.

I withdrew from all church-related activities. After struggling in private for several months I had an epiphany, a revelation of the grace of God. As a long term believer I had easily mouthed "grace" but somehow it was forever tied to the idea of "works". Well, for a considerable period of time I had done no "works"and had even been blatantly rebellious in spirit.

One snowy evening I was on my was home after a visit with my parents. Highway 14 was familiar with its small towns dotting the way before Wainwright. I was exercising caution as black ice was always an insidious peril. Shortly before the village of Irma, I felt the car slowly ease out of control and land in a snow-packed ditch, several meters from the edge of the road. It was close to midnight as I considered my *very few options*. With great difficulty I clambered up to the highway praying I would not freeze to death before help arrived. No cellphones yet. The era seems primitive now. When a half-ton truck came into view I changed my prayer to be safe from rape, death, kidnapping or maiming. On the side of the vehicle was the familiar logo of an oil servicing establishment in town. The driver was friendly and indeed I was safe. After dropping me at home I decided the car could stay in the ditch until arrangements were made to tow it the next morning. No damage was done during the episode and once it was safely back in the driveway, I made a quick visit to the business owner to thank him for his kindness in rescuing me. Perhaps it was an employee whose deportment was worthy of commendation. I was informed that they had no such truck and NO employee was on the road last night. I half-laughed, but did not give the satisfaction that I had lost my mind. Just commented softly, *"It must have been an angel"*. Exactly. I believe it was to this day.

Toward the end of November Douglas's 3 adult children and and I cleaned up the house and prepared a ritual of closure. It had not yet been sold, but I was moving into the future and away from Wainwright. We sat around the unique field stone fireplace with a roaring fire and shared happy stories. I had found an elegant bottle of champagne in the cellar. We decided it was a fitting drink to toast each other and the good future for all of us. Neil popped the cork and Ian took the first sip. He screeched, *"Don't drink it. It tastes like vinegar"*. Turned out to be a very old bottle that had not aged well. We laughed and decided there was a lesson to be learned. Do not postpone joy.

Emotions are tender and ragged when saying goodbye to a houseful of memories. I was prying my heart strings away from the dreams that had vanished while Douglas's children were bidding adieu to their childhood home. Different dimensions of a similar ache.

A Portrait in Progress

Communications skills can be unwittingly jerked askew. Two antique sideboards were in question. Mine (from the Eaton era) was stored in the garage as Douglas's exquisite oak piece was well-used in the White house. The oak piece deserved to remain in the family. However, no one took up the invitation to take it, so it was carefully loaded up and settled in a new home in Sylvan. A year later it was retrieved and re-settled in Sheila's residence. I had Dad's antique maple piece re-finished and moved it into our living room.

The six grandkids---Seamus, Alastair, Peter, Brian, Majid and Sabrine—all grownup now, would have delighted their Grampa Douglas's heart.

I need to remind myself every once in awhile I am a human BEING, not a human DOING. A vessel just has TO BE. I wasn't quite airborne, but I was on my way taxiing down a new runway. The future was mine. The shadows brushed in the canvas were waiting for strokes of brightness to make the picture beautiful.

Marriage to Kenneth

A PAINTER HAS reached an important stage in his/her work when the time for the first colouring has come. The painting has been "resting" awhile, silently preparing itself for further artistic skill on the part of the artist. The first colouring allows the element of surprise. The unexpected introduction of a new palette; perhaps a feathering in of an imaginative feature somewhere in a corner. Something that will make the picture memorable and unlike those that have proceeded it.

It is a natural phenomenon in animals (humans and otherwise) to develop and maintain a defense system when attacked. Even when there is only a perception of impending danger or hurt, the system kicks in with all available force.

I recall conversing with Dr. Kevin Hay a few hours after Douglas' demise. We were in our living room and my now late husband was lying in state in the bedroom. Trying not to fall apart in his presence I moaned, *"Kevin, I will never do this again. Giving away my heart in love is simply too risky"*. He hugged me and wordlessly comforted me.

Three weeks later I had lunch with a young woman I had known for years. We were discussing our lives. She was weeping because she didn't seem to have the ability to GET a man. I was shedding tears because I didn't seem to have the ability to KEEP a man!

One day in May of '94 I returned home to find the message light blinking on my answering machine. At first the unfamiliar voice was indistinct, but after listening several times I "got it". The gentleman on the tape was a first cousin of Jess, Kenneth Lynn. He was calling from Tampa, Florida where he was employed by Air Canada. Such a surprise! I had known Kenneth since 1965 when he had completed 5 years with the R.C.M.P. on Prince Edward Island. Over the intervening years we had been together at Lynn family reunions in Ontario. One summer before Jess died, he brought his oldest daughter Donna to visit us in Wainwright. The kids wanted to see a Disney movie at the local theater which happened to be within walking distance of the house. Attending a movie was an act which was considered verboten in that era for a Pastor's Kid. At the time, however, a bit of spunk lifted its head and hollered, "Who cares? If there is any fallout, we'll handle it". Off they went, happy as clams and no one had a word to say about it.

Kenneth was coming up later in the summer to spend his birthday with his identical twin Douglas (!) in Ontario. Could he make a detour to Alberta and have a short visit with me? Well, why not? A time was arranged in August, and I promptly forgot about it.

A journal notation for July 19 poignantly reveals some private feelings I never breathed to anyone.

> *Worked evenings on the Orange unit. Came home and came apart. I can't believe how lonely and sad I feel. When I compare my first grief experience I feel I am BEHIND schedule. I need a long hug from someone nice. I feel so vulnerable and needy.*

Losing one husband was a humbling experience for me. To lose a second proved to be humiliating. In a twisted way I felt if I had been more clever, more prayerful or endowed with great faith, perhaps the stats could have been altered. For 2 years whenever I was in the presence of someone new and had to reveal my marital status, I merely said I was a widow. If they were curious to know what my late husband did for work, I chose one or the other, depending on how high my humour thermostat was at the moment. I would reply,"*He was a clergyman*" or ..."*a family physician*". In some perverse way, it helped me stay intact.

One of the board members of the church lost his wife less than a year after Douglas' passing. His wife was a good friend and I missed her dearly. Stefan was a good man, honourable in every way, but a bit provincial. He would have married me in a trice. It was very difficult to gently tell him I did not feel the same way.

Mid-August arrived on schedule, and so did Kenneth. He flew into Calgary, rented a car and drove out to AL-VI-NOR. The red rental car drove into the driveway, I peeked out the bedroom window. WHOA---I had forgotten he was so tall and handsome. Maybe I should not have extended such a warm invitation! I had carefully arranged every hour of the next 3 days. Central Alberta is a great "show-off" place. We attended a dinner theater in Rosebud and laughed until our sides ached. After 2 heavily programmed days, he finally said, "*Could we stay home this evening, and just talk, please?*" Certainly. And what would he like to discuss? The grisly conflict in Bosnia or the pathetic state of Rwanda, perhaps.

"*Well no, not really. I would like to talk about...us.*'

Oh, oh. My angst jerked up a notch.

And so we began to talk. A torrent of words flowed out of each of us. We were 2 crushed souls communicating on a level that was deep, but mutually understood. It is more than apparent that no one lives a life without a few mistakes. If there is such a rare individual, I do not care to make his/her acquaintance. The pride emanating from their presence would be stifling.

In 1969 Kenneth married a beautiful American lady. There were irreconcilable challenges a few years later. They struggled on as parents of 2 little girls, but finally it became a situation that was no longer tenable. They divorced in 1988 and began to build new lives for themselves.

A trip back to P.E.I. for a charity golf tournament proved to be fortuitous for Kenneth. He reconnected with a woman he had dated during his tenure with the R.C.M.P. Her husband had left her after siring 4 children because his sexual orientation was not toward her. They healed together, regaining lost trust and allowing their hearts to open for a loving relationship once more. A move to Florida in January of '92 was prompted by a job offer in Air Canada for Kenneth. In September, Carolyn died of anaphylactic shock of unknown origin. It was a stunning blow that ended a cache of wonderful dreams for the couple.

With the support of family and a church congregation, Kenneth's wound slowly healed. I had written him a note of condolence when I heard the sad news but had not had contact with him since. (I do things like that!)

One of the things I found supremely frustrating about living alone was the propensity for things to warp, split or decay. My non-skills at house maintenance are legendary. I have been known to destroy items while endeavouring to repair them! When this handsome visitor fixed my aching vacuum, my admiration knew no bounds.

The time together ended and I made a mistake. I kissed him goodbye. Immediately my heart flipped. Somewhere deep inside I felt a paradigm shift. That isn't what I expected, much less desired. I was independent. I had a career, my sons did not need a father figure, and I was determined not to put myself in a position to be torn apart. No M'am, not me. Is the picture in focus yet?

I flew to Ireland and he flew to Ontario. Many months before I had booked a quaint hotel in the county of Roscommon. My goal was solitude amongst beauty for 10 days. I longed for a measure of settledness before plunging into my new career of chaplaincy. Sightseeing was a low priority as my primary objective was to sleuth out my adoptive father's roots.

Naturally the visit of Kenneth *severely* complicated my repose. A lot of reflection was done in my corner room which overlooked the ruins of an ancient abbey. One of the housekeepers was especially attentive to my every request (which were very few). She made sure I had coffee and cookies every afternoon at 3 o'clock. Mary was the epitome of Irish hospitality.

In the end, it came down to one of two choices. Either I could hand up (so to speak) a neatly organized plan for the rest of my life and petition the Almighty to bless the list as written, OR I could choose to sign my name at the bottom of a blank sheet and say, *"Here, God of the Universe, fill this in as You see best".*

I chose the latter, but promised myself I would not pursue this relationship if there was no letter from Florida waiting in my postal box when I returned. Seemed like a fair deal to me. For public information, there were...TWO!

When I arrived from Dublin on the return flight into Edmonton, I stopped in to see my parents before heading down highway 14 to Wainwright. I was weary from jet lag, but anxious to pick up 2 weeks of mail before turning into my familiar driveway. I stopped at the uptown Postal Station but in my haste neglected to lock the car in PARK. Somehow the gear landed in REVERSE, and in horror I watched the maroon Maxima slowly back up, no driver in sight. In full tilt panic I ran after it. It kept going *very slowly,* thank the Lord, but I was unable to grab the door and get inside to steer it. Then a miracle happened---. On its own it turned right and headed up 3rd Avenue. Huffing and puffing (high heels don't cut it in a race!) I kept running, all the while praying it would not strike another car or maim an unsuspecting victim. It glided up a deserted ally way as though it was guided by an Unseen Hand. Once again the vehicle made a deliberate turn and came to gently rest against the sturdy fence which surrounded the Alberta Government Telephone building. Regaining the driver's seat, I sat there for a few awe-struck moments reflecting on what had just transpired. No damage or scratches were evident on the car and only a slight, indefinite dent in the fence. I phoned the manager the next morning to apologize but offered none of the scintillating details.

Over the next few months we supported both countries postal systems as well as the phone companies. We kept our relationship to ourselves, neither one of us willing to admit love had come knocking again. An entry in October spells out the way it was.

A Portrait in Progress

> *Kenneth phoned at 12:45 a.m. he told me if he was awake, I should be too. TeeHee.*

My entry into hospital pastoral ministry was going well. I had found my niche. An upcoming convention in Montreal, which would draw chaplains from across the country, caught my attention. Two female colleagues and I decided to register. I pulled together enough funds to fly down with them. Rooming with them was a delight but the fact that Kenneth flew to Montreal to see me added a special glow to the whole episode.

It seemed so outrageous I was considering matrimony with someone who bore the same name as my first late husband. In an earlier era, I once supposed a hyphenated name had such a ring of sophistication. I could never figure out how to acquire one. When I married Douglas, the opportunity fell into my lap, I became Virginia Lynn-White. Nevertheless I must report it caused a lot of hassle because some folks do not know the difference between a comma, an apostrophe and a hyphen. Because I did not change it legally, I had the choice of who I wanted to be, depending on my mood. Merriment usually but suddenly I was faced with the scary possibility of Kenneth being addressed as Mr. White. I have had to explain to security people why my name is somewhat like my husband's...but not quite. I have actually received letters addressed to Ms. V.Lynn-White-Lynn which is too much to fathom. A few years ago I dropped the hyphenation to spare further nonsensical exchanges.

The time came to disclose to my 'initial" in-laws that their nephew was about to become their daughter-in-law's spouse. At first we felt rather anxious, but both of them thought it was a riot I would be back in their family, although technically I had never left. Douglas' children gave us a tacit blessing.

Confession is good for the soul. So convinced was I that this was the right direction our lives were taking, I purchased my elegant wedding suit six months before the engagement ring was on my finger. Faith at work, I'd say.

In February '95 I decided the time had come to register for Outward Bound, an internationally known wilderness survival course. I had a feeling it was "now or never". I was accepted and began to prepare myself physically for the rigors I expected. The following is an excerpt of an article I wrote once I was back (alive!) in civilization.

A dozen years ago a magazine article on Canada's "Outward Bound" spurred my interest. I saved the article in a file folder. Three adolescent sons made the adventure impossible then but this autumn THE TIME HAD COME.

For months after the registration was finalized, I believed everyone should expand their horizons and just do it! Three days into the course I was cowering in the bush wondering where I had laid my head when I decided to do this stupid course.

Originally I signed up as part of a personal journey that included a desire to learn new skills in an environment completely foreign to me. The discipline of "stretching oneself", as it is euphemistically called, seduced me.

It took only a few hours to understand how incredibly illiterate I am in the ways of camping. A bit late to back out after one has flown halfway across the country. Another thing—there is no such opportunity to be E-vaced out because of sudden despair at the ever present sand, the infernal dampness and the thought of no toilet facilities other than on-guard pine trees and snoopy squirrels.

The group consisted of 9 students and 2 instructors. A feisty co-ed mix of nurses, managers, financial consultants, a computer expert and a librarian. The age range was 26 to 64 years.

The corporate goal was to canoe south along the Black Sturgeon River to Lake Superior, a route of approximately 60 kilometers as the crow flies, NOT as the river loops! Included in the week was a day of rock climbing and rappelling as well as one 12 hour "solo" time in the wilderness, alone.

Try to understand the scene. Nine days, eleven people, five canoes. All the food, tents, and personal items were loaded into heavy duty backpacks that were packed, unpacked and re-packed every single day. Are you feeling tired yet?

The majority of the participants had little or no canoeing competence, myself included. Appropriate paddle strokes for the bow and stern were taught the first day which happened to have a wind blowing at slightly less than gale force. This was a complicating factor when combined with nausea. I did my best as a team member to be smooth, straight and swift. Muscles unaccustomed to these new movements were summarily ignored when they vented ill feelings in the form of merciless aches.

The rock climbing feat came on the 2nd day. Trust had to be quickly developed as my life depended on the steady hands of a new friend holding the ropes at the bottom of the abyss. On my descent from the top of a steep cliff my wristwatch broke as I lost my footing and slammed into the face of the rock. Its instant disability to tell time was another discipline for someone who is "tied to the clock" and all but compulsive about promptness.

We were allotted 2 rolls of toilet tissue. Please contemplate that fact for a moment. Let me clarify—2 rolls for the entire group for the entire week. A low, all encompassing groan arose when that announcement was made. On the 3rd day into the adventure only one roll remained. Not to worry our over-cheerful instructors informed us. We were to discover Ontario grows lovely thick moss which can be used in a multitude of ways. If I have any advice for a prospective participant it would be this. Wear a bra with triple E cups and stuff them full of Kleenex and tissue. At least you will have a secret supply of something deemed essential in a normal life!

Not once during those days did we hear about Bosnia,

O.J. Simpson or the Quebec referendum. Dare I say, did we care? Not too much. Our focus was learning to go beyond our former limitations and search out new personal potential There were days when I thought I would never make it home. The portages were so difficult over uncharted river banks that I just wanted to lay down and die. I figured I would be so maimed my prospective groom would cancel the wedding. The end sometimes does justify the means. I emerged stronger in very way. If I could drink river water, go without bathing or shampooing my hair for a week, I could tackle anything life chose to throw at me. In time I would call on this new found prowess to survive another kind of wilderness,

The river water looked pristine. LOOKED, that is the operative word. All of us dipped our mugs into the water that was declared safe to drink without any type of purification. HA! Three days after returning home I was gagging and hopping to the bathroom with remarkable speed. I suspected "Beaver Fever". After becoming severely dehydrated I was admitted to the Red Deer E.R. where the diagnosis was confirmed.

The year 1995 meandered on. As it did, somewhat of a dilemma arose. I had not said much about our upcoming wedding in November to friends. I suspect many of them were quite unaware of what was happening. In reality, I was afraid to let them know of my new found happiness. Perhaps I feared teasing (can't you live without a man?) or worse, scathing judgment of some sort. However, by the end of August I let the word leak out I was getting married again. W-E-L-L-L, I was unprepared for the excited reaction. Within one week some long time friends from Edmonton's Central Tabernacle planned a bridal shower for me. I was overcome with gratefulness . We had so much fun with all the gifts that young brides usually get. For instance I opened a dainty package and out fell ...a lacy thong! I put it on my head like a head band, pretending I did not know it real purpose. Hoots all around!!

How glad I was that I was totally mistaken in my assumptions of people's reactions. "Check out your assumptions" was added to my list of mantras.

We were married 6 weeks later in the newly dedicated transfaith chapel in the Royal Alex Hospital. I suppose one could say I was willing and Kenneth was brave! Rev. Dr. Neil Elford performed the ceremony. He included a tender symbolic act in which both of us "transplanted" 2 small house plants into a larger container of dirt mixed with ashes. It represented the potential of brand new growth and beauty rising up out of the ashes of disappointment and sorrow. Powerful metaphor as well as moving.

Kenneth wore the shoes he had worn at his other two weddings. It became a joke that causes titters to this day. Norma was my matron of honour as she had been twice before. On the morning of the big day she said, *"I am not doing this again for you!"* *"Me either!"* I assured her. Kenneth's twin brother was in the same position and I believe indicated a similar sentiment. Who could blame them?

Once the honeymoon in Hawaii was over, he flew home to Tampa and I drove back to Sylvan Lake. We had the marriage certificate on file, but for the present our relationship was to continue as a long-distance affair. Why be normal?

Finding My Genetic Background

I WAS FULLY aware of my adoptive status, inwardly certain of some kind of maternal abandonment, but lacked a pervasive compulsion to discover my "real" roots. Mom and Dad Thompson were progressive in many ways considering their generational upbringing. They did not cling to material things or ideas with pathological tenaciousness which made it difficult for those who loved them. They relinquished their home before illness forced them to do so. My father gave up his driver's license at 89, accident free! I never heard them whine about the massive changes made mandatory; for example, the metamorphosis of the beloved old cabin to a house or the inconvenience of losing a measure of independence.

One area they were loath to release was information about my adoption. In 1980 I persuaded a courtesy aunt to tell me the name of my birth father. When she said "Joe Green" I felt faint. She swore she knew nothing of my birth mother. There was no reason to doubt her word. A few years later Alice pulled out a nicely framed picture of my birth father, hidden away under her bed for 5 decades. There was Joe Green, dressed in his Air Force uniform, looking handsome and proud. Looking at his image face to face was a tender moment. My parents were in their eighties at that time and I believe were beginning to "tie up loose ends". They wanted me to have some clues about my birth parent, but I sensed they feared I would switch loyalties and love them less. Not particularly rational, perhaps, but I honoured their anxiety.

In March of 1986, just as I was leaving for the silver anniversary of my nursing class, they shared the news in a rather off-handed manner that Joe had died. I mistakenly assumed it was a recent event. The source of the information was never revealed. Upon returning from the celebration in Victoria, B.C. I wrote in my journal--

> *I'm in a real DOWNER. I admit I was ugly re: mileage money. Also the news of Joe Green's passing and the idea of having an older half-brother is absolutely depressing. It is though I have my own booing section.*

My adoptive father survived my mother by almost 2 years. I brought him down to the house at Sylvan as often as I could. It was his all time favorite place. One Christmas, after a perfectly lovely day, he died in his sleep. The moment of finding my father lifeless will never leave. I believe he simply released himself knowing he was cherished and in the place he had loved for so many years. He left life on his own terms.

The will was straightforward so I was able to do most of the legal work myself in preparation for probate. My parents had worded the document so no one would come out of the woodwork to snatch away any portion of my inheritance. The anxiousness about the possibility of my half-sibling never truly left them. Somehow I felt it was inappropriate or crass perhaps to initiate a search for my birth parents while Norman and Alice were still with us. Isak Denesen once wrote, " *To be a person is to have a story to tell.*" I knew there was a story in the shadows, but I was willing to wait until the time was ripe.

Kenneth encouraged me to initiate a search. I was curious, but not compelled. Unpleasant accounts of adoptees' torn emotional states until finding their natal roots were familiar to me. I did not want to be responsible for mauling a neatly organized family unit that had no idea I was once part of their parent's past.

Ever since I could reason things out, I had assumed my birth mother was either dead, or had been confined to a psychiatric institution diagnosed with postpartum depression. In 1940 the malady was considered a severe mental disorder. Often prolonged hospitalization was the only recourse. No sophisticated drugs or even intentional understanding existed. The barrenness of the unknowing was intriguing, but I could live with mystery.

Basic to all understanding and knowledge is the premise one begins with the known and moves into unfamiliar territory. Incidentally, the same concept holds true for artists. An idea takes on a life of its own once a a decision to create has been made. I mulled over all the tidbits of information I had about my birth dad. His name, occupation, musical bent, a move to Northern B.C., a second family. That was the sum total of data I possessed in order to move into a search mode.

I recalled an incident early in 1979, long before I had any clue about my background. One of the local churches sponsored a Ladies Night Out. I was asked to share some of my African stories. Being new in town I was still in the process of linking names and faces. The group's executive was remiss in not introducing me to some of the participants who had arrived around the same time as myself. I was nervous (cannot recall the reason for that at this moment). I plunked myself down at a table of friendly looking women. To break the ice, a silly little game was started. Everyone at the table was asked to repeat her own name as well as all the others. For some reason this heightened my discomfort. When my turn came, I introduced myself as "Virginia Green". I was so embarrassed at the goof, but somehow managed to pass it off with a laugh. The evening continued to diminish from that moment onward. From whence did that come? The only explanation is my high anxiety must have triggered some unconscious memory that flew out of my mouth in that verbal misidentification.

I made an agreement with my husband and a covenant with God that at any point of the search a situation developed which would spell distress, I would simply withdraw and feel satisfied with whatever information I had gathered.

A plan began to crystallize. During a 2 week vacation in May we would motor to northern B.C. To check out cemeteries and town hall records. I am bemused as I now reflect on our ambitious confidence. Closer to fervor minus insight, methinks!

As a preliminary gesture I wrote letters to funeral home establishments in Prince Rupert, Smithers and Terrace. I sketched out the meager details with one important condition. Under NO circumstances was the fact I was searching for Joe Green to be revealed to anyone, especially family members if any still happened to be in the vicinity. Thanking them for their cooperation and help, I waited for the replies. Six weeks passed before a terse note arrived from the Prince Rupert funeral home. Their records had been checked and no record was found therein... sorry for that. No letters were forthcoming from the other two establishments.

Kenneth and I began to plan our trip's itinerary. Our last stop would be in Kelowna where Jess' parents had resided since 1988. The time drew near for our departure date, and my apprehension began to grow in leaps and bounds. Northern B.C. suddenly seemed much more expansive!

I had a luncheon date with Marlyne Seemans, a pastor's wife who had engaged me to speak at a community outreach later in May. Briefly I shared my dilemma. For a moment she was absolutely still, and then softly said, *" I have a word from the Lord for you. Relax. Everything is going to be alright".* And right there, over a double fudge brownie in the middle of the Cheese Cake Cafe, she prayed for a portion of peace to envelop me. Highly unusual dessert time! My anxiousness melted away and the trip regained its glitter.

And then, a few days later...this journal entry says it all--

May 1—I just had the most incredible phone call---from Heather Green, Joe Green's daughter, my half -sister!! Mary , his wife, lives in Okanagan Falls, just out of Penticton. All their lives they have known about me. A feeling of euphoria has descended., I phoned K. right away, I know I sounded hysterical. Phoned Phyllis and Marlyne to share the news.

Finding My Genetic Background

I feel prickles arising on my hairline every time I review that journal entry. A series of providential moves took place with such exquisite timing which left no doubt the entire affair had been divinely engineered. A few days earlier, a group of people were enjoying coffee in a Terrace restaurant. A woman by the of Jenny had traveled down from Stewart for some family business. As the conversation progressed, a gentleman who worked for (owned?) the Scrader Funeral Home in Smithers, casually asked, *"Anybody here know a man by the name of Joe Green in Stewart?"* He then went on to explain this interesting request from some woman in Alberta looking for her father's grave.

Now Jenny happened to have a good friend by the name of Wanda Green. She promised she would inquire the next day after she returned home. True to her word she phoned Wanda to ask if by any chance her father-in-law's name was Joe. Indeed that was the case.

"I never met the man. He died years before David and I were married," Wanda replied, *"but I'll find out".*

Her husband David worked out of town in a gold mine, 6 weeks at a time. When he returned for a couple of weeks respite a few days later, Wanda told him about the Smithers encounter. Was he aware of a girl child from another relationship?

"Of course—I have known about her all my life," David answered. *"I even know her name! It's Virginia."*

Upon request the funeral director faxed David my letter and he in turn faxed it to his sister Heather, an accountant living in Nanaimo, Vancouver Island. Within 24 hours Joe Green's second family knew I was alive, well and searching for them. An awesome unfolding of a sublime agenda.

In one fell swoop our vacation itinerary was altered. No pressing need to scout out towns in a sweat bath of haste and angst. From conversations with Heather and her mother Mary, I discovered my birth father had died in 1974, a date considerably more distant than I had imagined. He was buried in accordance to his wishes, in a remote cemetery on the side of a mountain.

David's work schedule required him to be back at the mine

during the time Kenneth and I were planning to be in northern B.C. As a consequence the proposed trip to Stewart was postponed until September. However a mini family reunion with the other members was organized by Mary to coincide with our vacation.

Rearranging our holiday was easy. On May 16 we drove from Kelowna to Okanagan Falls. My mouth was parched from apprehension. A few kilometers from our destination I wondered outloud if curiosity had preempted wisdom. Only when I saw my new "old" family streaming out the front door to enfold me in welcoming embraces did I finally relax. Over coffee the questions and answers went back and forth like pistol fire. Mary was only 12 years my senior, a Salvation Army lassie by profession. Five children, 3 boys plus 2 girls, were born to that union.

Mary was eager to share stories of the good and bad times she shared with Joe. The good times happened when his skill as a cook was in demand. The bad times included months when the only living space was a converted hayrack with the cooking stove outside. I was filled with admiration for the grit and pluck required for this family to survive. I thought their life teetered on *awful* after hearing all the survival tales. When I shared my stories of widowhood, life in Africa and so on, they figured my life had been pretty gruesome!

Joe was a creative innovator in his own way. He made sure his family never felt the sting of poverty. In reality, his 5 offspring never felt anything but blessed. One summer he contrived a pool-heating device from a discarded oil barrel. Copper tubing was rigged up the inside while a fire burned in the middle. An ordinary garden hose was attached to the copper tubing and BEHOLD, warm water for his children to splash and enjoy.

One story moved me more than the rest. Mary explained Joe mourned the loss of me until he died. Somewhere during the years of separation he lost touch with Norman and Alice. It remains an enigma who told them about his passing. I wasn't astute enough to gently pry further information from either of them. They took a few secrets with them to the grave, and that was one of them. I can rest without knowing.

Mary went to a linen closet to bring out a picture of me. I felt my chest constricting. It was identical to a photo which hung on my parents' bedroom wall for as long as I can remember. It now adorns a wall of one of my sons. Evidently Joe would take it to an upper attic and weep with remorse. He never quite reconciled the fact he had given me up for adoption. A number of years previous the family had made an effort to locate me on the strength of a rumor I had moved to Vancouver Island. I cannot imagine the origin of such an untruth.

When we drove away, my head was swirling with novel possibilities. How different would my life script be had I remained within the confines of Joe Green's care? Mentally I tried hard to see myself with these new friends within the parameters of "family". They were gracious and welcoming which I appreciated more than words could express. A grateful heart reiterated my thanks for the loving provision of the Thompsons.

In what way could this encounter impact my life? Certainly the information about my birth father's demise from colon cancer had genetic significance for the monitoring of my health. On that premise a colonoscopy is a regular "every 5 years" ritual. It has important ramifications for my sons, but it is a bit harder to persuade them.

I required quite a few weeks for this newly found family connection to be woven into the fabric of my psyche. I was advised to visit Stewart B.C. before the end of September. Snow comes quickly to the mountain range in that area. I did not wish to delay a quiet closure at the grave site of my father. Accordingly, I made plans, this time without Kenneth as he was unable to accompany me due to a work schedule.

Traveling to Stewart, which houses Canada's most northernly open harbour was an adventure. On September 30, 1996 I "hopped" from Calgary to Vancouver to Terrace by air. An inhospitable layover in the town's "bus depot" (a misnomer, trust me) awaited. In an effort to hang on to a sense of groundedness, I walked and wrote journal entries. A couple of these notations now seem entertaining but at the time I scribbled them, amusement didn't seem to fit my general outlook. Casual conversations with friendly customers told me it was mushroom picking time. I needed to be on the lookout for the harvesters along the highway to Stewart. Well, one learns something new every day. Mushroom pickers who sell their bounty for high returns? Never met one in Alberta! I kept that in mind as a decrepit van, petitioning the heavens to make everyone think it was a bus, pulled up and the driver asked for passengers to Stewart to identify themselves. Here are my hand-picked notes of that ride.

12:45 PM. I have prowled the SKEENA MALL. Had a great walk over a long bridge. It is a magnificent day. Did I mention there were 3 quality stores that gave me no end of pleasure? I tried on lotions, sampled perfume sprays etc. until I must emote enough fragrance to influence anyone however I fancy!

5:45 PM. I walked back to the mall and bought 18 gorgeous roses. I am now on board this pseudo-Greyhound bus. We are roaring (speed and sound!) thru' this most wonderful territory. 2 guys and me—we comprise the entire passenger list. One of the men is acting like a stand-up comic. He has just spilled his liter of red pop. It is flowing down the aisle and he is meticulously mopping it up with bits of paper. The driver is trying not to look and frown. He steadfastly steers this contraption down Highway 37. I gave him a Kleenex to help with the mess. Very grateful, he was. He is wearing tight jeans with Wellington boots. Sure hope I don't need it any time soon...the nose tissue, I mean. Oh oh, the other guy just yelled, "STOP"---there are my friends, the mushroom pickers. I have to get off". Pulling the bus into a halt, the driver obliged. I couldn't see a soul, but then, maybe I wasn't looking in the right direction!!

There are more tears just under the surface for this meeting than for the one in OK Falls. Possibly because I have thought about going to my fathers grave for so many years. I really do not know what to expect from David and Wanda. I hope they do not think I am intruding on their life.

The kind bus driver dropped me off at David and Wanda's—one of the advantages of knowing everyone in a small setting. My uneasiness faded in the warmth of their hospitality. The next day we drove around the town and he introduced me as his sister. I was touched by that reference. We stopped by many of the places he and our father spent long hours fishing and hunting. We arrived at Ward's Pass Cemetery around noon, a forlorn, unkempt place. I deliberately withheld any judgmental feelings to myself. In addition to the roses purchased in Terrace, I also had a small candle scented with apple-crisp fragrance. It was symbolic as Joe was known far and wide for his superb apple crisp desserts.

The flat gravestone was clean with the neatly chiseled lettering easy to read. I laid the roses out, fan-shaped. Placed a small altar of rocks to hold the candle steady, sat back...and wept. For myself, because I felt "gypped" he left this world before I made his acquaintance. For Joe himself, because of the woundedness he must have felt deep in his soul. For my mother, whoever she was, and for the excruciating pain she suffered because of his insensitivity. David stood a respectable distance away with his back turned so my grief was private. The wind was bitter in its fierceness as we left the graveyard. Neither of us spoke for a long time during the drive back to Stewart.

I returned the next day on the same shabby vehicle still hoping to be classified as a reliable means of conveyance. The driver told me when he was a kid in school, the classes went over to the Green house for field trips. The fine collection of cats, fish and other pets was considered an education in itself.

Autumn came and went as autumn always does. My new position as a chaplain on the Palliative Unit required energy, creativity as well as compassion. Thoughts about finding the other half of my parent couple faded temporarily. In January of '97, reality came knocking with robust vigor. I remembered a commitment to speak on Mother's Day at the Beddington Assembly in Calgary. Interestingly, the senior pastor had requested me to be present for their Mother's Day celebration the previous year, hoping I would dwell on the theme of adoption. I demurred, saying I wanted to wait until I did further research into my own personal situation, but promising a firm date the following year.

Suddenly a deadline loomed. I had a serious chat with God that ended with a plea. *"I need INFORMATION RIGHT NOW. PLEASE AND THANK YOU."* The information I had at my finger tips was less than minimal. Figuring I had nothing to lose and possibly a good deal to gain, I contacted the Alberta Post-Adoption Registry in late January. This department, under the auspices of Family and Social Services, acts as a bridge between seeking individuals. If both parties inquire about matters of adoption, a connection can be arranged. I knew my mother's maiden name was Bice , her given names, Evelyn Lorraine. This information was gleaned from a zeroxed copy of the marriage certificate kept by Joe Green's son David.

A kind reply from a Mr. Keith Owen on the 12th of February contained this statement--

> *Please be assured your application has been placed on file and in the event of registration by another interested person, a representative from this Department will contact you to discuss the matter further.*

No one ever looked for me??!! How depressing. The slump passed and more than ever I knew I was waiting for a miracle. Not one to sit back and twiddle thumbs, I scoped telephone books in a number of Alberta cities. In Edmonton there were 2 listings of the name Bice. As it turned out it was a mother and daughter duo. The older woman had been recently widowed and expressed some measure of surprise there was a possibility of another branch of the Bice family living in this province. Her late husband had never mentioned any relatives with their rather uncommon surname.

The miracle came in the form of...Mary Green. She phoned one snowy morning and asked my permission to try and locate my half brother. She recalled meeting him once before she and Joe married. According to her somewhat fuzzy recall, his name was Roy or Ray, the last name either Green or Lawley/Lawson. A hunch told her perhaps he resided in Penticton. Could she do what she had to do in order to find him? Well, why not?

On April 5 I arrived home from a visit with Kenneth feeling harried because of a delayed flight plus a flat tire on my way home from the airport. The indicator light on my answering machine was blinking informing me a message was waiting.

> *Hi Virginia. Its Mary. Your mother is alive, She lives in Campbell River. B.C. Phone me right away, okay?*

The need to sit down immediately was urgent. Such stunning news. Naturally within moments Kenneth and all my sons knew this critical bit of news. I wandered around the house dazed as I unpacked my suitcase and tried to absorb the implications of having a living female parent I had assumed was dead. An entire day passed before I had the strength to call Mary for further details.

She had indeed located Roy Lawley. During their initial conversation he assured her he also was aware of my existence. In fact, on several occasions he had made attempts to find me. Shortly after chatting with her, I phoned Roy—a sort of "reconnaissance" call, checking the waters, so to speak.

He put my anxiousness to bed by assuring me our mother wanted me to phone. She was probably sitting by the phone at that very minute, waiting to hear my voice. Evelyn Lorraine lived with my half-sister Ella, born in 1943.

I made the call an hour later, sipping a cup of herbal tea and praying to be brave in spirit. The conversation was, understandably, a bit halting. Both of us tried very hard to keep the tears from garbling our voices. My mother's voice reached out and hugged me over the wires. I knew I had to fly to Campbell River as soon as possible. The next day I booked a flight to her town. The support I received from the nursing staff at work was overwhelming. The memory of those abundant best wishes warms me still.

A Portrait in Progress

There is a scribbled entry on April 11 in my travel journal. On that day, the flight from Vancouver International Airport included a quick stop at Comox before touching down in Campbell River.

> *5 p.m. I have kept myself busy with other thoughts. Currently reading "Finland on the Cheap". Have landed and taken off from Comox. I am already crying---seven minutes to Campbell River Seven minutes to the unknown. I have taken 56 years to get here. It feels like a surreal experience. Am I there yet?? There is a woman across the aisle who keeps looking at me—I wish she would STOP THAT!!*

When the plane taxied to a stop on the tarmac, I was the last to leave. The flight attendant asked me if everything was okay. I must have looked like a wreck, but I managed to perk up and reply brightly, *"Yes, sir, everything is just fine."* By some generous gift of grace I managed to disembark without falling. Ella stepped forward to greet me and then led me over to the bench where our mother was resting. I cannot adequately describe the next few moments so I won't even try.

Over the next few days all of us laughed and wept together. I was aware of how painful my appearance in Evelyn's life must have been. I honoured her discomfort by limiting questions to general areas of interest. We would have more time in the future to pursue difficult questions, or so I thought.

One inquiry was posed as soon as an appropriate moment opened. Was there a history of breast cancer in her family? None of which she was aware. Sigh of relief. Another journal entry--

> *Mother has had her gallbladder out, a hip replacement and recent cataract surgery. She is so perky and has a marvelous sense of humor. As we gently dredged up memories she spoke without rancor or meanness. After she heard I was coming for a visit, she crocheted me an aphgan. It is beautiful.*

Purple, pink and green. Guess what???? Her favorite colour is purple. Is that genetic or what?

Her parents had 2 sets of twins. A coincidence as Joe's family also included 2 twin sets. Coupling these facts with the Lynn genes that also had the propensity for multiple births, what chance of escape was afforded me? I was doomed, metaphorically speaking!

I mentally stored tiny pieces of trivia. Mother loved seashells, peacocks, lemons. She used to bake voluminous batches of cookies, and then hide them in ingenious places. Her amazing ability to remember exact dates was uncanny.

Ella related to me a recurring dream that plagued her for years. She dreamed she had found me in northern B.C. but before we had a chance to know each other, I rejected her. The thought of being rejected caused Ella many moments of distress.

When I flew home the next day, there was the anticipation of a late summer visit at AL-VI-NOR. A brief stopover at Kelowna was arranged to bring the latest news to my in-laws. I also wanted to have the opportunity to meet Roy and his wife Elaine. They drove up from Penticton and ferried me to the airport. Over coffee more pieces of the backstory fell into place.

Roy also had a recurring dream for years. In his dream he saw a man walking a small girl to a large meeting place and offering her up for adoption. Meaning eluded him until we met face to face. Are you getting goosebumps yet?

I was back into reality within hours of flying back to Sylvan Lake. I pondered the significance of recent events. How would these encounters impact my life? Certainly the lack of diseases which are predominately genetic in nature was a comfort.

In August of 1997, mother, Ella and her husband drove out for a three day visit. I introduced her to my world. Jaxon Jesse, Regan and Tracey's newborn son (my first grandchild) was only 2 weeks old. I could not read the message in her face as she cuddled him close to her heart.

A Portrait in Progress

Late in December of that year I wrote an article which was subsequently published. Here is part of it.

> The debate about nature versus nurture is remarkable in its inconclusiveness. How much of who I have become do I owe to my birth parents and how much of the equation is tipped towards my adoptive caregivers? My genetic parents gave me the gift of life, but the two saints who adopted me showed me the path of life.
>
> Some of the things I do by rote because over the years I watched Alice Thompson do them that way. To be brutally truthful, I DO NOT do certain things---simply because she insisted! It is a theme which has been in existence down through the ages.
>
> It is a balmy December night (an oxymoron if there ever was one for the citizens of this fair province) as I crank this out. An hour ago the sad news arrived via a phone call my birth mother is dead. She slipped away peacefully in her sleep, just as we all would if the choice was ours.
>
> Sadness surrounds me like a long flannel scarf. Thank God I did not procrastinate that initial "getting to know you" visit. Equal gratitude for the strength provided for the trip to Alberta late last summer.
>
> My life's view was expanded by meeting this woman whose constant companion was brokenness. How did this reunion impact both of us? I would like to believe our coming together helped restore some of the happiness my mother deserved so much in her sunset years. More than that, it has convinced me there is no such thing as a terminal mistake or an irredeemable entity in God's economy.

Kenneth and I flew out just days before Christmas for her memorial service. It was a joyless, soul-dulling affair which made me sadder still. We were the odd couple apparently, as no one seemed to know of my relationship to Evelyn Lorraine. There were uncomfortable stares as we made our way to the front row in the Kingdom Hall. The officiant's message seemed aimed at those present (us!!) who were not in the fold, as it were. Nevertheless we enjoyed a good time of fellowship at the local Donut Shop after the service.

According to Jonathan Stephenson, who has written extensively on the material and techniques of painting, a second painting adds details and further modifies colouring. It is worthy to note this technique refines the picture gradually whatever has already been done. This is the essence of the stories I heard .

Employment Termination

THERE ARE SOME things I just KNOW, and act accordingly. Resigning from nursing, moving to Sylvan lake, and entering into chaplaincy can all be considered as acts of faith. Toward the end of my initial unit of Clinical Pastoral Education, I set up an interview with Fabian Marshall, the director of Pastoral Care at the Red Deer Regional Hospital. I offered myself as a volunteer in some pastoral capacity. He asked me to describe my idea of a dream volunteer position. Then he pressed me for a description of a dream JOB. Except for the money, they were much the same. I was thrilled when he said, *"Come on board. This facility is known for creating positions for volunteers who have good ideas and who are willing to work to fulfill their dreams."*

    I did exactly that. Volunteering on the ward designated for palliative care allowed me to orient myself to the staff and the expectations of the hospital. I was in Tampa, Florida completing my second unit of C.P.E. when the letter from Fabian arrived confirming my new job, a part time position as chaplain on the palliative unit. I started employment on September 4, 1996. Having an office with my name on the door was so invigorating. The décor was definitely cosy. It looked more like a living room, and therein was its strength. Staff as well as the patients and families came in and felt at home.

    Attendance at a new employee orientation was mandatory. One

morning, 5 weeks later, I was sitting in the current session which explained the "nuts and bolts" of the hospital facility. During the first coffee break I was approached by Mr. Lathrop, the C.E.O. of the hospital and one of the vice-presidents of nursing. They informed me Fabian had been injured while felling a tree and was now hospitalized on one of the medical floors. Would I considering "covering" for him until he was back at work?

Such confidence they had in me! It was a lovely affirmation of what I knew I could do. The next 5 weeks were busy as not only did I have the palliative unit to cover, but also the entire hospital. There were lots of challenges but no disasters during that time.

It had been part of my routine to meet with Fabian every Tuesday at 10:30 a.m. to discuss work. Initially these encounters were mutually beneficial. When Fabian returned to work in mid-November, I noticed a slight shift in his attitude toward me. Not much, mind you, but enough that when I walked out of his office, I had a sense of disquiet.

I had written, at his request, a list of goals for myself. They did not seem to satisfy him so I rewrote and prioritized them. I was chastised for not including patients enough and told to delete the goal of meeting every department head in an effort to become more acquainted with the inner workings of the establishment. Fair enough. I revised the list once again. I concentrated on the items that were categorized as "high priority". Those included regular "Care for the Caregiver" sessions with the staff, helping family members in the anticipatory grieving state, guiding patients in life reviews, journaling and so forth.

Christmas of '96 found me "on call" for one week. Life at the hospital was fine, but my own life was 'stress city". Regan's wife was hospitalized on December 23 for a severe bout of asthma-triggered pneumonia. High doses of intravenous antibiotics had been administered to stem the infection. Under normal circumstances this would not be a cause for anxiety, but Tracey was in her first trimester of pregnancy. Certain antibiotics are tetragenic (harmful to unborn babies) and THAT was worrisome.

It was the first anniversary of my father's death. I needed a slice of solitude to re-group and contemplate. Because of my work schedule I was not getting much of either. On the morning of Christmas Eve an unheralded family crisis blew my peace on earth away. Somehow my intuitive self had not picked up the signals. As if that wasn't more than one lady could bear, my credentials with the church organization with whom I had served faithfully for 33 years were being stripped away because I had married a gentleman whose "ex" was still living! I pulled myself together to minister to patients and families who were in more serious straits than myself.

When the New Year began, the director of Pastoral Care did not seem overly interested in my broken heart. In retrospect, how healing a pastoral a prayer or two addressing the hurt would have been. All new employees are on 6 months probation. I knew on March 4 I would be given an evaluation of my work. I wasn't the least bit worried because things on the ward had been going well. Fabian asked me to prepare a self-evaluation to discuss with him. No problem. I outlined what I considered the "pluses"--the bereavement program was in process, my office was proving to be a safe haven, the sessions with the nurses were lively and varied. The "minuses" were also there—regular memorial services had not yet been commenced, little or no progress could be seen on the proposed new palliative unit.

The diary entry for that day explains what happened when I went to his office.

> SHOCKER!!! I went bouncing into Fabian's office expecting my probation evaluation----and he won't be giving it to me until after I have a appointment with an audiologist. This is HASSLING!!

My probation period was then extended another 6 months until October. I was stunned. My hearing impairment had NEVER been discussed before in that context. To be put on a further time of probation (not counting my year as a volunteer) was incredibly hard to fathom.

I made an appointment with an audiologist, not just a hearing aid salesperson. During the time of the thorough examination I said very little about the reason for the appointment. She saw through my evasive answers and remarked, *"This man is threatened by you. He'd like to fire you!"* Her directness caught me off-guard, but the import of her words seemed remote. She wrote a detailed report of her findings to Fabian.

Part of her letter is as follows.

> *Ms. Lynn-White has reversed sloping hearing loss which is atypical for fitting amplification. It has been my experience that it is very difficult to fit amplification on reversed sloping hearing losses as we tend to over amplify the higher frequencies and therefore drive the patient "nuts" with noise.*
>
> *She is an excellent lip reader and is very effective in using environmental manipulation techniques and communication strategies. I would recommend that she continue on this path as opposed to pursuing amplification at this time.*

Unfortunately, Fabian was highly dissatisfied with the report and continued to insist I either get hearing aids or my job was on the line. He did some research on his own (Wikipedia, perhaps?) and wrote a letter to the audiologist contradicting her knowledgeable work. She was furious. It was an affront to be assessed by an obviously out-of-touch individual on a subject about which he knew nothing.

One suggestion which seemed to ameliorate his fussing was the idea of a pocket auditory device. I henceforth carried it with me whenever I was on duty, but the results were poor. The nursing manager, Cheryl, was dismayed when I explained my situation. She reminded me it was contrary to terminate an employee just because of a disability. Besides, she had never considered it a problem so what was Fabian's hidden agenda?

Toward the end of April I received a letter written to the management of the hospital. Mr. Lathrop gave it to Fabian, who in turn

A Portrait in Progress

passed it on to me. Hindsight tells me it must have galled Fabian to do so. It was a letter from Dr. Kenneth Strand, a professor at Andrews University in Michigan. He appreciated the excellent care he had received following a freak accident which required his hospitalization. He went on to write--

> Another aspect of your care program that I especially want to comment in this letter is your Pastoral Care Department. Chaplain Virginia Lynn-White visited me several times and had prayer with me. This was most helpful and encouraging.
>
> As an ordained clergyman myself who in my parish ministry and as a seminary professor have made numerous hospital calls on the sick, I am deeply appreciative of your healing program. If Chaplain Lynn-White is typical of your entire Pastoral Care program—and I assume she is---I must rate that program as absolutely superb.

Suddenly the hearing impairment was no longer a pressing issue, but several other elements began to darken the horizon. First of all, my credentials as a licensed minister with the Fellowship of Christian Assemblies were no longer good enough. I had to be ordained. Worthy of note---in my contract the words "accredited minister" were used. I had transferred my credentials "horizontally" to this organization after the Pentecostal Assemblies of Canada had seen fit to remove my name from their list. Each faith fellowship has its own parameters for ministers. The F.C.A. did not ordain women or men who were not actively employed in parish ministry. Hey, did I care if I didn't have the title of Reverend? Not too much! In actuality my new ministerial license gave me more privileges than my former group. I was now recognized by the Alberta government to marry.

My pastor, the late Rev. Elmer Whittaker, thought the idea of me not being seen as "accredited" because I lacked official ordination was simply ridiculous. He wrote Fabian confirming my standing with the church. The missive was dated May 27, 1997.

This letter is to confirm that Virginia Lynn-White is a member of Living Stones Church and has been licensed with the Fellowship of Christian Assemblies. If you have any questions regarding her licensing, please do not hesitate to call.

The next issue was my further education. I was working on finishing my Bachelor of Theology degree. I was wrapping up a course called Expository Preaching. The pressure increased overnight to finish it IMMEDIATELY. In the midst of mounting anxiety I stepped up my studies.

Further to that, more intensity was brought to bear by the insistence of my completion of an advanced level of C.P.E. One of the components of my contract read as follows:

In addition, admission by the Accreditation and Certification Committee of the Canadian Association for Pastoral Practice and Education to advanced training towards Specialization or its equivalent (minimum of 2 C.P.E. Units) is required. Full certification as a "Specialist in Institutional Ministry" is preferred, and candidates without such certification must be prepared to pursue completion within five years of date of hire.

I was only 7 months into the position but had already contacted Rev. Dr. Martha Rutten-Wallis who had agreed to be my consultant when I took my 3rd unit of C.P.E. at the Tampa General Hospital. Rev. Dan McRight had written to assure me he would supervise me in the spring of 1998. Everything was set, but Fabian insisted I take the unit in the summer of '97. I felt uncomfortable about being away during the summer of that year when my first grandbaby was about to make an appearance. Besides, I had 5 years, that is until 2001, to obtain my standing as a specialist. I fully intended to pursue that course of action.

One by one I endeavoured to meet the hurdles, but the tension escalated. There were no written (or verbal, for that matter) complaints that I was aware of. Fabian had never "shadowed" me all during time I worked on the unit-- –until 3 days before my termination.

Nevertheless, the stress quota grew daily. Many of my diary entries in June are simply "STRESSED OUT' page after page.

I had an uneasy feeling the day he told me he was going to come with me when I did my rounds visiting with the patients. One of the patients was an elderly woman, severely deaf, who was slowly easing out of this life. I bent down close to her ear as I whispered a prayer of comfort. I could feel the air stiffen as we left the room. Fabian admonished me *"Her relatives didn't know what you were doing when you bent down to her".* Okay, I guess I should have explained my reason. I promised to do better next time.

The next patient was a family friend of my supervisor, not terminally ill, just in need of an encouraging word and prayer. After a few moments of chitchat, I invited us to gather in a circle and hold hands during the prayer. WELL-----evidently that was verboten in Fabian's view. I knew I had 2 strikes against me!

Earlier in the year Fabian had asked me to cover for him the entire month of his summer vacation. It seemed incongruent he would want me to fulfill those responsibilities when obviously he believed my work was inferior. One day I asked him to clarify his position by the end of June.

On June 26, he did exactly that. At a luncheon meeting with fellow chaplains, he asked me if he could meet me at 3 p.m. With savvy and clarity (and a touch of boldness) I asked him if he could come to my office, my comfort zone.

Precisely at the appointed time he arrived. I was handed an envelope, business-sized, regular, white. I laid it down on my desk, unopened and allowed him to continue 'chit chatting ' as a pretense of serious engagement. My heart experienced a chill when a few moments later he succinctly delivered his message, *"I am terminating you".* I had recently watched the movie "Jerry Maquire' and managed to say quietly, *"Show me the breach, please".* In other words, what have I done wrong?

Somewhere along the line he had decided my caring was not compatible with the Red Deer Hospital's approach to pastoral care. I requested information in which it was clearly stated what the hospital's philosophy of caring was detailed. At that time, none was forthcoming. With a sweep of his hand, he informed me I had a week to clean out my office. I must admit that was a kindness for which I was grateful. My world, as I had envisioned it, lay at my feet shattered.

I sat looking out the window, composing myself for the hours and days which lay ahead. Picking up my pen, I was granted the grace and peace to write a note to the president of Red Deer College, Dr. Dan Cornish, who at that moment was dying of a rare kidney ailment. Word spread quickly and within 30 minutes 3 management nurses were in my office offering support and solace.

Reaction from the staff was quick and angry. Confused by what appeared to be a mindless act, the staff became very resentful of the pastoral care department in general. I requested an exit interview with Mr. Lathrop the day after Fabian had scheduled his final talk with me. My level of trust had been totally destroyed. In order to protect myself, I asked a member of the Employee Assistance Plan to sit in on my interview with Fabian. I had written down concerns I wanted to raise and over the 30 minutes allotted to me, most of them were addressed.

I had in my possession letters of support written within days of my termination. Two of them were copies, originally addressed to Fabian. Excerpts from one written by a staff nurse, Louisanne, are as follows.

> *I am shocked and deeply opposed not only to her dismissal, the manner in which this action was taken. I find it painfully obvious that Red Deer Regional Hospital's philosophy of caring and theology of practice must not extend to those who have given a huge piece of themselves to the service of making this facility a better place. I am ashamed to be to be associated with a facility that would find it necessary for whatever reason, to treat someone with Virginia's integrity and passion with such disregard.*

A Portrait in Progress

The doctor who was the physician liaison for for the palliative care team was very supportive. He wrote Fabian after a "statement" was read to the staff which supposedly answered all the likely questions. He kindly sent me a copy and I have his permission to include the following paragraphs.

> *This "statement" has caused me some problems. In it you do not really deal with the matter raised in the letter received by Virginia. In the "statement" you mention first her hearing. When I heard of this concern I was completely taken by surprise. I had never once realized this was a problem for her. You stated that she could "fake it". I would rather say she compensates remarkably well.*
>
> *The matter of ordination appears to be an issue that also should be resolvable. If her present faith group licenses her but does not ordain her because she is not in a parish ministry, it would seem to me that is a question of semantics that should be able to resolve. In terms of her pushing her particular values on people, I just do not think that is true.*
>
> *My final concern is that I would have hoped these apparent concerns could be resolved better in a Pastoral Care Department. This situation sounds like one that might arise in a cut throat office where the bottom line was profit, not people.*

In the weeks that followed June 26 it was difficult not to allow anger at the injustice permeate everything I did. I made an appointment with an attorney, not for the purpose of litigation, but rather to get an informed opinion of someone who was not emotionally involved with the situation. I brought all the letters and documents which were relevant. In a few days I received a response. Her letter was 3 pages long, much of it explaining the legal aspects of an employee on probation. Alberta law allows the termination of such an employee without an explanation. Of interest is her view of the situation.

> *Based on what you have told me, and the documents provided to me, Rev. Fabian Marshal has done nothing legally wrong. However, there is an over-riding sense there is something ethically or morally wrong with the handling of your employment and termination. It appears that Rev. Marshall was neither supportive nor helpful. His comments in his June 9, 1997 letter in which he offers his continued support and willingness to help appears to have been a hollow statement. This is particularly shocking to recognize from a member of the ministry, whose very work is based on helping others.......*
>
> *It is interesting that you perceived a change in attitude from Rev. Marshall after his return from his injury. I too would personally question whether he felt threatened or diminished himself by your apparent success in fitting into the hospital environment and the positive relationship developed with staff and patients alike.*

In time, of course, I began to see clearly that what had happened, no matter the hidden issues, was a case of injustice. It became evident I needed to have some kind of closure with the staff who were grieving and in need of some kind of pastoral care themselves. We decided to have a dinner party at Monsieur Wong's in central Red Deer. Over egg rolls and fried rice I tried to explain my feelings. As professionals we needed to think long and hard about our roles as advocates when someone is being disempowered by another person. What could we learn from this situation that would help us grow? I encouraged them not to let this disappointment terminally affect their attitude towards the pastoral care department. One man does not comprise an entire ministry.

The servers were getting anxious to close the restaurant, but many of us lingered over numerous refills of coffee. As we were saying our goodbyes, one tearful nurse asked me if I could let burned-out caregivers come and rest at my home in order to help them recover. I hugged that small comment to my heart as I began the 30 kilometers drive back home. Admittedly I was a menace as I steered the Saturn over Highway 11A, tears trickling down and a nose that needed blowing. By the time I reached the "S" curve of Birchcliff Road, I too had turned a corner. The healing process had commenced. I suddenly saw the possibilities of a retreat for folks with crushed hearts. Details were faint as the idea took shape on the drawing board of my imagination. I just KNEW I could figure this new venture out, given time and grace.

Summer breezes brought new creative energy. In September I wrote an article I hoped would be published. The editor of the magazine decimated it with blue editing marks adding he wanted more paragraphs on the "happy ending". Well, I had no idea at the time how happy the ending would be! I am including it here as it gives a window on another aspect facing those who happen to find themselves in the bin labeled "unemployed".

Up From the Ashes of a Firing

Maybe its called a firing because of the intense hot flush one feels immediately after the news comes down. Hey, that is a gender-neutral feeling! Perhaps its because in an instant one sees the ashes of a bright future suddenly appear as a mental image. Maybe its the rush of rage that accompanies the realization an injustice has just happened, and it has been us on the receiving end.

My primary career was nursing, enhanced with specialty training in midwifery. Mentally I flipped back to a former era when I was in labor for the first time. BREATHE. Oh yes, I had forgotten how important that was. Breathe in. Breathe out. I coached myself to let the indrawn breath go. "Keep taking in oxygen," I thought to myself. "One does not expire if there's enough oxygen around."

The first reality check came when I remembered I had bought a great pair of walking shoes 2 weeks previously. Seemed like such a prime idea then. Not so much now. Should have saved the money. Then another realization. I had just plunked down my VISA to pay for a winter-caused "boo-boo" on my car. The $975 was due soon. Could

I have not borne the ugliness of a bumper-bash just a bit longer? Apparently not.

A vise suddenly attached itself to my heart.

A moment later I recalled I still had 4 cans of tuna left on my shelf plus a bunch of pasta and lots of tomato sauce. I could go on a diet of brown bread and cheese. Cheap but nourishing.

The vise thing kept on squeezing.

There is a peculiar humiliation about being terminated. It was as though someone had driven a spike through the frontal area of my skull, and left me dangling, a spectacle for all the world to gape at and titter. I thought I would die. Naturally I did not. Instead I went into mourning. All the dreams of financial stability, the opportunity to set the gold standard for chaplaincy on the palliative unit were lost. I released them one by one.

A week later I had my exit interview. To prevent any possibility of misinterpretation of words, I asked another employee to be with me. The dialogue went as I had anticipated and I left feeling disconnected and hurt.

As I left the hospital that day, a young woman was smoking just outside the entrance. A sign proclaims that kind of behaviour is not to take place there. It irritated me beyond degree that she was wearing a dress similar to one hanging in my closet AND being so blatantly disrespectful of the hospital's guidelines. She stubbed her half-finished cigarette on the sidewalk and started toward the entrance, deliberately bypassing a receptacle specially made for smoldering butts.

Turning toward her I said pleasantly, but without a smile, "There is receptacle for cigarette butts," pointing to it. This remark was met with a bearish glare, but I walked ahead and ignored it. I was about 2 meters away when I heard her spit out, "Slut face". I have self-censored that the remark as I do not want to contaminate this page. I continued walking, laughing to myself. I had heard her perfectly, and somehow, the exchange made me feel feisty.

The stress triggered by the loss evidenced itself in physical symptoms. My left leg became painful and wobbly. I limped, no matter how slowly or carefully I tried to hide it. I suddenly encountered the "triple S syndrome'--difficulty in speaking, sleeping and swallowing.

During the weeks following "T Day" I was good to myself. Foot massages became part of a regular routine as well as weight training. I ate sparingly but in healthy fashion and dropped 7 pounds. I lit candles as soon dusk fell and sought solace with close friends who cried with me.

I made the initial trip to the regional Employment Insurance office. Roseanne the counselor was helpful in her own way. I noticed at once her suede fuchsia shoes and wondered what kind of a salary grid she was on. All the questions. All my vague answers.

"What kind of employment will you be seeking?" Roseanne kindly interpreted that as "What do you do?"

"I'm a chaplain. I mean, I was a chaplain. It's like a pastor to people who are dying, and their families."

A long drawn out "Oh-h-h" was the response. Then a big silence. I imagined her thoughts chasing each other.

"W-e-l-l-, what would you LIKE to do?"

"But, you don't understand, I loved my job. It was...a calling." Intuitively I know have chosen the wrong word.

This is a public place. I feel like everyone is aware of my confusion. Is my face crimson with embarrassment?

She replied softly, "There aren't too many openings for that kind of thing. What else can you do?"

A very long pause ensued. I had retired from nursing 2 ½ years previously and with no active R.N. registration, I could not get a job in a hospital. Besides, I did not want to be a nurse anymore!

"Surely you can do <u>something else</u>", her voice intruded my musing.

Brightening up I replied, "Oh yes, I give seminars on stress management, bereavement preparation, grief recovery—things like that."

Roseanne frowned. "Hmmmmmm—that's considered self-employment and we really do not count that".

Suddenly I felt anemic. Probably looked it too. "Lord, whatever is *going to become of me?"*

The most bitter day came a month later when a letter arrived stating I did not qualify for EI benefits. I was 57 hours short of the required time. This was a nasty revelation. I had paid E.I. premiums for years, then took off 2 years to further my education. In that time frame, the government changed the rules. An absence of 2 years meant a person was considered a new/young worker and was required to work a certain number of hours before qualifying for benefits. A great sense of betrayal on the part of the Federal government swept over me. In my most cynical moments, I wondered if the director of the department who engineered my termination had known this fact and deliberately timed my exit to inflict a second sorrow. I'll never know for sure.

One learns new things in a time of squeeze. To be sure, they comprise old bits of knowledge, but now, they are stunningly relevant.

1. Life can be unfair. A person can work/live like the Virgin Mary or St. Francis, and if someone higher up the chain of command has unresolved issues within themselves, one can consider themselves toast, kaput, finished---choose your term.

2. Forgiveness is an important component in maintaining integrity and spiritual growth. The process needs Divine assistance, but it is possible.

3. Creativity is often birthed in the crucible of adversity. Out of my brokenness, my retreat center for people with broken hearts was established. I have a few credentials for operating such a place that were not taught at college.

Now on this side of my pain, I understand why God allowed such a catastrophic event to happen. I would have never moved on from my cherished job. My ministry continues. It just happens to have a different venue.

****

A few weeks later I was scheduled to speak at a Women's Ministry conference in Edmonton hosted by my former faith group. Several of the national executive were in attendance during one of plenary sessions. The chairwoman asked the executive members to join her the front of the auditorium. An invitation was given to some of the participants to come and pray a blessing over each of one. Rev. Bill Morrow, General Superintendent at the time, stood to one side, looking a bit forlorn when no one came along side to pray with him. I hesitated for a moment before deciding it was the perfect time for me to initiate personal forgiveness for the brokenness caused by the abrupt withdrawing of my credentials after serving the organization for more than 3 decades. Rev. Morrow represented the entire denomination. I stood by his side and asked God to bless him in an unprecedented manner. Returning to my seat, I felt a fresh lightness and knew I had chosen the right path.

One of the terms used to describe a particular type of paint is referred to as "body colour". Generally this means the paint has been made opaque by the addition of white. It becomes thicker; more skill is necessary as it is laid down. One author on the subject of early Flemish painting refers to its characteristics as "dense". On reflection of the preceding situation, the terminology is not wholly out of place.

The Retreat at AL-VI-NOR

THE ACHE OF the job loss was ameliorated on August 2 by the birth of our first grandchild, Jaxon Jesse. This infant's birth, over whom I had spent countless hours in pre-natal worry was to become a defining moment. Looking at his darling countenance (isn't that what all grandmothers say?) reinforced the belief my family was the most important motivating factor to live long and well.

Ten months later I was present at the birth of Mackenzie Summer, grandbaby two. Would you like to see a picture of her? I heard my son Rael welcome her into our family when she was barely 5 seconds old. Instantly I was overcome with a feeling of regret. Jesse was not present for any of our sons' births and suddenly I ached for how much he had missed. Inwardly I wailed at how much our sons had missed the first "father bonding". Then I was struck at how much I had missed by his absence.

Autumn's glorious days were nectar to my soul as the edges of my heart "granulated in". I spent considerable time reflecting on the questions *"What in my life is calling me?"* and *"Why pretend it is not there?"* I knew I had to pick up the pieces of shattered dreams and build something new. My passion was ministering to people who in some way had been bruised by the harassment of life.

A Portrait in Progress

Surveying my premises with an eye to operating a retreat for folks in need of respite was an enlivening exercise. Obviously the hand of Providence had played an impressive part in the original design agreed upon years before. The loft upstairs with the bedroom, private bath and tiny Finnish sauna, plus the atrium with many house plants made a perfect combination for guests who needed peace, privacy and solitude.

Once I made the decision to leap into entrepreneurship, many decisions had to be made. Primarily I had to obtain permission from the council governing the summer village in which I reside in order to run a business. The bylaws state "No commercial enterprise is to be set up within the boundaries of the village." Once my letter of application was received, a 3 month delay ensued as the officers polled my nearest neighbours to see if any objections were raised. None were forthcoming.

The next step was to register the name. My adoptive father had designated the name AL-VI-NOR years before when the property had been purchased. It was a compilation of our names, Alice, Virginia, Norman. I could think of no other name which would be as meaningful, so it was duly registered with the government. I laugh when I recall how many times I have been asked what language it is!

In October I was bold enough to return to the E.I. office to visit one of the managers. I needed to be assured there was no other appeal process I could pursue regarding the disablement of benefits. Diane was wonderful in her encouragement as she told me about a program for people wishing to begin a business of their own. I didn't really qualify, but the rules were about to change again. Perhaps I had a chance. She gave me permission to "drop her name" with the person in charge of this particular area of training. Within a week a phone call from her confirmed I was accepted. I started classes a few weeks later and emerged with confidence and creativity ready to commence my new venture.

I was encouraged to compose a "Mission Statement" which would succinctly tell the world what AL-VI-NOR hoped to accomplish. It reads as follows--

> *AL- VI – NOR will provide an atmosphere of peace which will facilitate guests to begin their own journey of self-healing, fully aware of the essential aspect of their spirituality.*

I reflected on some basic "internal quality' questions. For example, "What could I DO?", "What could I NOT do?" and "What did I NEED to do?"

I decided I needed to proceed with plans for my third unit of Clinical Pastoral Education to qualify for advanced standing. Along with this I applied to St. Stephen's College in Edmonton for the Masters of Theological Studies program. Suddenly a Master's degree held much more allure than a Bachelor's! I had the capacity and gifting to welcome those whose lives had endured a rude interruption. Facilitating "soul work" seemed like a natural part of my personality.

Embracing reality helped me acknowledge I was not a gourmet cook. In fact, I could have been the co-author of the *"I Hate to Cook"* cookbook! Fortunately for everyone, people in crisis want food that comforts, and please, forget the mango souffle`.

I cannot accommodate several guests under normal circumstances due to space restrictions. However, sometimes unique situations prevail and guests have an indoor camp out with sleeping bags placed wherever a comfortable spot is found. I cannot harbour (as part of my professional accountability) anyone with active suicidal tendencies or those with abundant mental issues which are pathological to themselves and others. With a sober sigh I admit I am "developmentally diminished" when it comes to mathematics. That is a big "OOPS" in the life of a business-person!

As I moved along the path of healing, I knew there was another item I needed to finish. Forgiving Fabian as well as my former ministerial colleagues for a lamentable lack of pastoral presence when it was most needed, was proving to be a process like I had never forged through before. It took several months of prayer and soul-searching before I had the courage to go to the office of the director of pastoral care in the hospital. I also drove to the office of my former presbyter, now pastoring a church close by. Both men had acted with such avoidance, one could be forgiven for believing I had been afflicted with Hanson's Disease once the news of my credential stripping was evident. I needed to tell both of them I forgave them for acting in such an obvious anti-pastoral fashion.

I should have left well enough alone. Neither of them were very gracious as I opened my heart and explained the reason for the appointment. Between them they lobbied the following questions/statements at me---all irrelevant in my opinion. I answered as best I could without flinging back a number of questions/statements of my own.

> *Are your children serving the Lord?*
> *Do you have anything in your heart against me? (X2)*
> *I hope you didn't take it personally!!*
> *All that kind of stuff comes down from the district office (an unwholesome attempt to shift blame to someone higher up).*
> *Well, I guess if this has been bothering you, its best to reconcile it.*
> *We are all in recovery, you know.*

Tears threatened to leave their place of abode as I explained how I envisioned forgiveness. It does not restore innocence. However, it does restore a measure of integrity to a wounded relationship. I shook hands with each of them and blessed their ministry as I left.

I got in the car with the distinct feeling neither of them "got it". I drove out of the parking areas and muttered to myself, *"Beauty is only skin deep, but STUPID goes all the way through!"*

I'll admit that was redundant and irreverent to boot, but it lightened the moment. More than anything I longed to hear them acknowledge my pain and say something like, *"Thank you for having the courage to come here. What can we both learn from this?"*

Lynn Johnson, creator of the wildly popular comic strip *"For Better or Worse",* once wrote, *"An apology is the best glue. It can fix almost anything."* Anything that remotely resembled an apology would have been a welcome relief. It did not happen.

Very few alterations to the house were needed. A sacred space was created in the upstairs gathering room. A gorgeous stained glass window, designed and executed by my sister-in-law Betty Wood, was installed in one of the French doors leading out to a balcony overlooking the front lawn. The area was replaced a few years later with an atrium which affords year round benefit of sunshine. I scouted antique/specialty shops for suitable furniture to complete the ecumenical chapel space. A baptismal font from a closed Presbyterian church, a small hand-crafted pew from Quebec, a long unused prayer bench from an Anglican house of worship and a unique communion cabinet from a United Church finished the sacred space in grand style.

The loft, the chapel, tiny sauna, inviting guest room, atrium—all together they were pronounced perfect. My family gathered with a few close friends, along with my minister for the purpose of celebrating this new venture and sanctifying the entire venue with a blessing. It was a hallowed time.

Just before I left for my third unit of C.P.E. at the Tampa General Hospital, I had my first "test run" with a guest. Actually, 2 sisters-in-law with attached problems. I flew down to Florida with wings in my heart because the encounter with these women affirmed to me I COULD DO THIS.

I worked *very hard* to achieve advanced standing the next 3 months, but not before having one of the most unpleasant encounters with a gentleman who was called in to "advise" each of the participants in my group. He was not the regular supervisor or even my assigned consultant. During the mandatory interview he proceeded to harass me on a number of issues based on some written work submitted to him before the day of our meeting. His tone and body language were so derogatory I left feeling totally forlorn. I walked out of his office, but my heart needed a wheelchair.

One memorable event in Tampa remains as a delicate reminder how fragile life can become in an instant. I had spent some time with a grieving family after their daughter had been brought to the Emergency Room, fatally overdosed. My beeper went off informing me I was needed in another area. I rushed to the treatment room where the medical staff was working on a homeless man who had been shot in an attempted robbery. An unusual feature about this patient was about to become a REAL panic situation. The gentleman was wearing 2 dozen gold chains--the objects of the thieves' desire-- and refused to let the staff remove them so appropriate treatment could commence. He explained through a voice of pain he had no place to store his treasures, so he wore them. The nurses re-positioned him in order to inspect the gaping wound. The movement triggered a massive hemorrhage which decreed immediate surgery to prevent a total loss of blood. But one cannot go to the O.R. with jewelry, remember? Not even wedding rings. Try to imagine the panic as those necklaces were unclasped and removed. Be assured those fasteners were tiny, not door knob in size. By some miracle they were all removed, tangled up and smothered in blood. An orderly and I were assigned to count them and put them in the hospital safe. I wonder if he survived to wear his booty again.

I came home the end of May, and within 3 days a client began a month long stay. My assumptions, which huddle on the periphery, include one that assumes everyone has the answer to their current crisis within themselves. Just because a person cannot "see it", does not invalidate that principle. My task as a pastoral person is to facilitate an empowerment of hope.

The guest-clients who came to my door often feel a few turns south of hopeless. Possibly even just 2 miles short of crazy. I quickly understood the task at hand was not "to fix". The best I can offer is to walk a short way with them through their pain. At times it may be extended. It was a wise decision not to advertise widely. Because I was alone much of the time due to Kenneth's work schedule, I took referrals only, or those who have heard about the facility by means of a friend.

I accepted a speaking engagement in Wainwright designed to

celebrate "Nurses Week." Briefly touching on my new career as a retreat owner/operator, the spark of an idea grew into a fire in the mind of one of the attendees. I had worked with Dianne for 15 years during my time in Wainwright. After the banquet she rushed up to me asking if it was possible to bring several nurses to AL-VI-NOR for a retreat. Why not? I would arrange a theme and a plan for a day or two of real retreating. Depending on the number of retreatants, the women could bring their own sleeping bags and snuggle up in any corner that pleased them. When they arrived several months later I was taken aback by the amount of food they brought to share. One large ice chest was laden with wine bottles and beer cans (all full, you must understand!). WHOA----I thought this could very well be my last retreat ever! This initial foray into group retreats ended well. We were so busy engaged in spiritual conversations the "bottled" spirits were all but forgotten. The core participants of that group have continued to bless me for 17 years...and counting!

One client, Darice Rose, experienced an epiphany while trying to feel settled in the small Finnish sauna. Raised in an uptight religious family she left her home province to train as a registered nurse. She was management material and soon found herself in various positions of authority in the health care industry. An offer to "move up" to a job with a corner office was tantalizing. The plump new salary grid was tempting but the move meant less family time. She arrived needing a quiet space in which she could consider all her options and the attached ramifications.

Sitting in the heat, inhaling the scent of cedar she suddenly had a flashback to her pre-school days. She recalled picking beans under the eagle stare of a grumpy grandparent. The blazing sun made her dizzy and faint. In a primitive effort to revive herself, she lay down in the shadows of the tall bean stalks. Grandpa disapproved of her perceived laziness and gave her a smack to emphasize his point.

Immediately Darice KNEW she could not accept the job opportunity in spite of the grand perks. Her realization came as a reaction to the hot sauna. She remembered with clarity her extreme aversion to a

A Portrait in Progress

desert-like climate. The city she was considering is known as an arid hot spot in Alberta.

Many of the women who grace the retreat are angry. A multitude of reasons present themselves as they begin to share their stories. When I sense an aura of authenticity--telling the truth even if it causes shame to rise--I feel the pathway to healing has been cleared enough to start the process. Anger is one emotion women have a difficult time wrestling to the ground. One assumption I personally had to release, but not before a protracted trashing, was that anger is counterproductive. I had been taught it was a sin. A really HUGE one.

This belief shackled my own spiritual expansiveness and ability to be helpful until I realized, with a knot in my navel, that assumption was a LIE. I took an intentional review of my own reaction to the person who terminated (such a ghastly term!) me without a reason that was valid to anyone except the fellow who lived inside his head. I called the emotion what it was, named the pain—*white hot anger.* Part of the energy to rebuild my shattered spirit came from the release of the anger. In the end it was used as a healing force.

I have learned to go beyond my boundaries -boldly- by incorporating liturgy and ceremony which are dictated by the needs of those who seek refuge at AL-VI-NOR. A number of years ago I had a client from Ontario stay with me for a week. This woman was mourning a multitude of long-standing losses. Abandonment, abuse, financial depletion, betrayal—you name it, this woman had been there, suffered that.

Together we designed a ceremony which would hopefully serve as a bridge to new hopes and life. She listed all her losses in black ink. Can you believe she filled 5 pages?!! On other sheets of paper she wrote the items she wished to reclaim in gold ink---3 pages this time around. We discussed the biblical principle of "jubilee" as found in Leviticus 25 and 26. Other passages in the Bible regarding restoration, that is to recover or get back, were studied. We bought a bottle of red wine to signify the sacrifice of Christ. On our last evening together, a cozy fire blazing in the fireplace, we lit a candle with 3 wicks, invoking all of heaven to be present—in particular, the Trinity.

After a prayer of anticipation, she cut up the pages inked in losses and dropped them into my best crystal bowl. When the last piece of paper fluttered down, we poured the wine over them and stated those losses were now covered by the redemptive power of the blood of Jesus. She then waved the pages with the items written in gold and said, *"In faith I take back all those losses. The years that have been eaten by sorrow will be given back to me."*

We poured the rest of the wine into exquisite glasses and toasted the future. Then we....LAUGHED! Wonderful, belly-tickling spasms of joy. It was a divine moment. The next day she flew back to Toronto , said a resounding "YES" to a man who asked her to marry him 20 years previous, and hasn't looked back since. She has phoned several times since then with a voice that has taken on the lightness of release and joy.

An article I read a number of years ago (my apologies to the author whose name I have forgotten) drew attention to the number of times –187 in all—the concept of "stranger" was used in the Bible. Reading that information had a profound effect on me. I began to see the idea of being a stranger as a metaphor. God issued some pretty rigid guidelines for the children of Israel to follow with their interfacing with strangers, even those considered unfriendly. Strangers were to be treated with respect, possibly given room and board if the occasion called for it. Many of my guests are strangers as I have never met them before. I have to provide an atmosphere of trust as they struggle with personal dilemmas. According to Scripture, I have a responsibility like no other.

Ah-h-h-h, from midwife to the laboring to mid-wife to the dying, and now a birth coach for the crisis-stricken. Indeed, I have come a long way.

A master painting often employed a technique known as *hatching* which involved making strokes and cross strokes in wet paint that blend together when viewed from a distance. It creates a compelling crispness at times while maintaining an interesting textural surface. Various life encounters offered me the choices I needed to fulfill my calling. A life that is not boring whether studied close up or from a distance.

Investment --- Identity Capital

ADJUSTING TO MY status as an unemployed chaplain fused with a hopeful retreat operator encouraged deep reflection. What did I have to do to accomplish the purpose for which I was born? Standing in the hubris of disappointment without the gallantry to move forward was not an option. I needed to improve my autobiography! Expand my resume! Embrace the possibilities of a yet undisclosed future!

I am amazed when I reflect on the contours my spiritual journey has taken. The line of movement was not in my imaginings as I stood as a young bride in 1965. Not one twist or graveled patch can be counted insignificant. I am today who I am because of where I have been, what I have done and the choices made at appropriate times.

The term *"identity capital"* was first described by sociologist Ames Cote in her book *"The Defining Decade"*. It represents our collection of personal assets. In other words, the repertoire of individual resources we have assembled over time. A person accumulates education, travel narratives, employment chronicles, family and relationship histories, grief episodes, joyful circumstances and so forth. Nothing is wasted or considered redundant. Everything matters. Every experience and encounter I have endured or enjoyed has enhanced my preparedness for the future.

I bundled up all the credentials I had earned (nursing, post-graduate obstetrics, theological college, C.P.E. Units etc.) and submitted an application to St. Stephen's College in Edmonton for admittance into the upcoming Master of Theological Studies program. Apparently the admission committee was satisfied with the information. I received a letter of acceptance shortly thereafter. Completion of the requirements for the degree became my 2000 millennial project. I signed up for the required number of courses and began planning my thesis. The goal of convocation in the fall of 2000 sweetened the accelerated pace of course assignments and the deadline for the "integrated study ".

The experience in its entirety was life-giving in a multiple of dimensions. Occasionally when a nostalgic spell touches an afternoon I delve into my essay assignments. It affords a minor break in real time when I am enveloped with a sense of "other worldliness"...*this stuff was really part of my landscape years ago!*

One of the professors was the loving father of a severely disabled pre-adolescent daughter. He sat with us for a week teaching "The Theology of Suffering". His own personal agony covered him like a finely knit shawl tucked around his entire persona. We watched the movie *"Lorenzo's Oil"* (Nick Nolte, Susan Sarandon) and held onto our heart strings as the father lamented his way down a curved staircase. One day we were required to choose a meaningful place, claim the space for a couple of hours and compose a poem about our own suffering.

Rarely in my life had a poem ever emerged from deep within. I did not know the difference between anaphora and cadence! However, if I wanted to ace the course, I had to come up with some kind of offering. No computer was available to Google *"How to Write a Poem in One Afternoon".* I noticed some of the other students looked a bit jaundiced at the suggestion.

The University of Alberta Hospital was within walking distance and without a moment's hesitation, it became my venue of choice. Both my late husbands had undergone treatment there. A suggestion to revisit the site brought an ache of sorrow, but after all, that was the whole point of the exercise. I have included this poetic offering as an example of what can flow from a heart that is allowed to tell the truth from a different perspective. For your information, I received a rating of 8 out 8 for my efforts! I believe the instructor cared more about feeling than form.

OBSERVATION OF SUFFERING IN FIVE SENSES

Here I sit, close to the entry point of my personal
Gethsemane.
My task today? To look loudly, so to speak, but remain hushed.
Memories swaddle me, covering the vestiges of grief.
Close to the North entrance there is a table
of jewelry for sale.
Watches--$20.00. Guaranteed for one year. Really?
Is the guarantee transferable to the patient in 5C3--
the one stricken with Lou Gerhig's disease?
Rare spindle-cell sarcoma, metastases, 4th stage cancer
Gruesome words, all of them.

There goes a faculty physician, a stethoscope doubles
as a necklace.
It trumpets her importance (to whom, I boldly ask).
Are the caregivers party to the care receivers?
The chapel is on the fifth floor. Whose brainchild was that?
Ridiculous site for a sacred space!
It needs to be close to the E.R. so relatives can rush there after being
summoned to hear of the fatal accident.

SIGHT
A Lottery Booth near the Food Court is a visual reminder-
Life is a lottery. In the end, we all lose.
Metis, Oriental, Black, White, Brown or otherwise,
Suffering is never colour blind.

Here comes a woman in her mid-time of living.
Pale face (naturally), dark hair (artificially) with a feeble smile
Trying to integrate both into the complex stages of suffering.
Does she realize her days are numbered?
If so, how far along are her plans to embrace each one?

Oh God, the woman with the raven hair, the deepset brown eyes,
She looks like-I can barely stammer it out- a former friend
whose betrayal gouged my soul.
My heart is in a reverse tumble.
She walks out of my sight, unaware of the distress I feel.

SMELL
The washrooms are close to the elevators.
YIKES! My nose perceives cleanliness has vanished in a flush!
Add the whiff of antiseptics, analgesics, and anesthetics.
One now has a balm –
capable of excoriating nasal passages.

HEARING
The bleeping"bleep,bleep" of the glass-walled elevators
could drive one who is close to the edge—
straight over and down.
Up and down, down and up, repeat repeat repeat.
The doors open to belch out their contents in
various stages of suffering.

TASTE
I needed something. Comfort was a far away entity.
I chose coffee. Mixed the Irish Cream with the Macadamia Nut.
Triple milk, no sugar.
It was the most outrageous act I did all day.
Finished the last drop. Tasted disappointment of a grave prognosis.

TOUCH
Moving from one area to another
I chose to sit in quiet corners, alone, forlorn.
Each chair I picked felt hard, unyielding, uncomfortable.
As one sits on the perimeter of the enclave called " suffering"
the overriding impression becomes, life is hard.

In this place of suffering,
Can I see God, smell God, hear Him?
Reach out and touch the Almighty? Taste His goodness?
Sometimes I wonder.

Millennial celebrations were rich and varied in the year 2000, also nicknamed Y2K. I added another personal one to my list of reasons to rejoice in that unique year. Contacting the government of Ireland, and dutifully following instructions, I was granted the privilege of an Irish passport. It was a gentle nod to my adoptive father's Celtic heritage. I have used it twice while traveling in the E.U.

Right beside the festivities there were suggestions of the imminent end of the planet. Fear that the electrical grid would rupture or a worse fate would descend in the form of an asteroid curdled the anticipation of some people. The Lynn family had our own reasons to celebrate. Two new grandbabies were to be added to Jess's legacy. Grandpa and Grandma (John and Edna) were in their 60th year of marriage and we as a family wanted to commemorate the occasion with them. We planned a party for mid-August. The car-port was gussied up, a caterer engaged and friends and family from near and far were invited. A day before the big affair, Hannah made it known she was unhappy (!) about having to wait to make her appearance. Regan and Tracey were at the hospital welcoming her while the rest of us observed the Diamond wedding Jubilee. Her great-grandparents had a visit with her just before they left for Kelowna.

Six weeks later in the midst of a group retreat, Rael phoned to inform me Leanne was in labour and could I please come to the hospital right away? Well, sure I could! My guests were all sleeping as I slipped out the driveway on my way to the Red Deer Hospital. Jarrett emerged a short time later yelling that it was much too bright and chilly in his new world! My daughter-in-laws are a source of marvel to me. All of them were eager to get up and get out of the hospital setting ASAP. I was eager to stay within the confines of the hospital and rest a while after giving birth.

October 2, 2000 arrived in the middle of the baby joy. It was the end of a 2 year life-giving journey culminating with a diploma with the designation of Master of Theological Studies. My goal was met and I was proud. Not enough to be *really sinful,* though.

Several months passed before an idea began take shape. I needed further instruction in Spiritual Direction. I had been engaged in this type of ministry for a long time, but never formally acknowledged the fact. I began to search for a program that would meet the need and at the same time be challenging enough to keep me excited about the possibilities it offered. Researching various venues and programs close to home i.e. Canada in general and Alberta in particular, proved to be a disappointing endeavour. At that point in time the possibilities were either scarce or rigidly bound by religious tradition. None provided the spark for a creative "rush" I needed to pursue a further round of studies.

I leaned into a time-validated principle. Once a decision has been made--my responsibility—events begin to unfold—divine intervention. Circumstances work out given the gift of time, usually in surprising ways. And so it was in this situation. A 2 day personal retreat at KingsFold offered me the opportunity of meeting new friends. Among the women who were present were a couple of Calgarians, newly minted spiritual directors. Both were edging close to retirement from their respective careers. A program entitled "Sursum Corda" had motivated them to explore the possibility of becoming spiritual directors. The course was sponsored by the Episcopal Diocese of South Carolina. No sooner had we engaged in conversation I noticed a distinct—how can I describe it without sounding totally ridiculous?

--physical cardiac response. My heart was saying *'YES YES"* in the only manner available to it!

I followed their suggestion and applied for the 2002 session. It proved to be a life-giving decision. The regimen included written assignments as well as 2 week long residencies in South Carolina. What an eye opener lay ahead. I was the only Canadian as well as the only evangelical. The participants were an interesting conglomeration of priests, laity, military, volunteers, all at various stages of personal and spiritual growth. All were required to have some form of counseling in order to qualify for the final certificate. True learning experience indeed!

The venue for the residency was a campground not far from the ocean's face. The atmosphere was spiked with salt foam, cockroaches and pelicans. The first week coincided with the sad military incident of a "friendly fire' killing of 4 Canadians by American troops. Naturally, I wore my aching heart on my sleeve and expected a bit of sympathetic understanding from my new American friends. Not a word was forthcoming. I was miffed and rather nonspiritual to boot. When I mentioned my feelings to the director she was loving and non-judgmental. She explained it wasn't included in the news in that part of the country and probably no one was even aware of the tragedy! Small comfort.

I read the following quote tacked up on a friend's fridge some time ago. She was unable to recall the author or the article so I ask forgiveness in not being able to give credit where credit is due.

> *A spiritual director is not a leader but a guide. Her ministry is discernment of events, and of liberation, enabling individuals and communities to move towards freedom. She may give them love, but not her thoughts, for they have they own. She may house their bodies, but not their souls for their souls dwell in the house of tomorrow. Through her love, silence and prayer, she seeks to be a light for those who search.*

A Portrait in Progress

I learned during those months of instruction the most life-giving aspect of spiritual direction can be described as a gentle invitation by the Holy Spirit to a person of faith to "go deeper and farther" along the pathway of growth. Andrew Marr points this out succinctly when he wrote, *"If we do not allow God to make us more than we are, we can only become less than we are".* In other words, we are wise to intentionally seek to become all we have been designed to become. This sacred task can be facilitated by a person "called" to be a spiritual director.

This interpersonal relationship can, by its very nature, become a bit inconvenient at times, which of course mimics all ministry. I see *availability* on the part of the director as a valuable characteristic. Naturally there are times when I would rather play with my grandchildren than attentively listen and receptively labour in prayer for a hurting, confused somebody who happens to trust me.

The entire world was shocked into mourning with the unforeseen events of September 11, 2001. Despair perhaps is a more profound description as most of us felt deep within our spirits nothing would be the same again. I was with my 6 sister-in-laws in a timeshare in Quebec when the twin towers came down. Our "girls only retreat" came to a smoldering stop as we watched the devastation on buildings and lives unfold before us. To prevent a total sense of aggravation that our time together had been spoiled by heartless ruffians bent on their own death wishes, we planned an outing which included a shopping jaunt in nearby Magog. I still wear an elegant outfit I bought that day. The pain of the over-riding event has not completely fled.

I am a member of Living Stones Church in Red Deer, Alberta. The church is a non-denominational branch of the Fellowship of Christian Assemblies. The leadership accepted my ministerial credentials (licensed minister) several years previously. The designation as such allowed me to perform marriages, but the process at that time was a bit tedious. I needed to be officially *ordained*. Each church within the organization is responsible for deciding which individuals meet the criteria for ordination. I saw no roadblocks so I approached the senior pastor, Dr. Paul Vallee about my desire.

"*Of course you can be ordained*", he assured me, " *I will present it to the board of elders and let you know*".

I have a couple of journal entries which betray my impatience with the time it took before the process was implemented. Not many women have acquired ordination in this denomination and I wondered if my gender was a factor in the delay. Apparently not.

The written assignments—personal spiritual journey, theology of ministry, statement of vocational leadership and so forth—along with the interviews were dutifully organized and accomplished over the next year . On January 19, 2003 I became Rev. Lynn ! In actuality, the name on the document reads Rev. Virginia Lynn-White. Allow me a small digression. Around this time, Kenneth had been addressed as *Mr. White* more times than he cared to remember. I decided to drop the hyphenated surname once and for all. It is part of my story but times change and every once in awhile a modification of some sort helps ease a rough patch.

The dynamics of blended families seem like a subculture of a hitherto unknown planet system. Checking my recall apparatus I find no mention of the highs and lows ever mentioned during a pastoral discourse. Considering close to 50% of our country's population find themselves in similar circumstances, that is an unholy shame. A letter arrived in the post box one day that suggests not everyone understands another one's heart. The address was incorrect and Sylvan Lake was misspelled, but the letter carrier delivered it regardless. The writer signed his name. Whether or not it was a pseudonym, who knows? Who cares?

> HELLO,
> *I see you around town each week and I wonder if you are a gold digger and have married so many times for money. Did you get a big money settlement with each marriage? Is that what you are holding out for now again? I am sure there is money to be had at the end of this run also.*

> *My sister-in-law stayed at your place a couple of years ago and we wonder if it is all paid by the government and you are reaping benefits. Think about what it looks like to us that do not have a great place at the lake. Even if it was your father's to begin with as we have heard.*
>
> *You do not deserve to have a third husband, but then money has a way of making monsters out of people.*

I have chosen not to include the *really* nasty bits in this discourse. Blending families is an art in itself. It becomes a creative act requiring heaps of love and an armada of patient understanding. If one partner has to work in another domain, then the challenge becomes more acute.

Our fused family did not include small kids as primary kinfolk. This of course eliminated the rigors of deciding discipline methods, support issues and the like. The grandchildren began to accumulate on Kenneth's side of this merger. Samantha Emily arrived on a sunny day in California to brighten the home of Larry and Donna Haynes. A little sister Kennedy Lauren followed 4 1/2 years later. Cameron Foth was born while we were enroute to Springfield, Missouri for a visit with his parents, Traci and Chris in 2001. Chloe arrived on Aug.17, 2003 and Noah was born on Sept 6, 2005 making "Three's Company" a reality in that household.

We are blessed by health and available resources to be able to plan itineraries which include our own beloved country in addition to places beyond our borders. Both Kenneth and myself have been dusted with the shimmer of "wanderlust". The love of travel can be compared to a hardy virus---difficult to shed with no known medications to relieve the symptoms. Spontaneous take-offs may be exciting, but usually astute pre-planning helps circumvent disasters, real or imagined . I keep the following *"Lynnsight"* (originally printed on May 22, 1991) and some what modified, close at hand when musing about an upcoming trip.

> *The best advice I ever heard about traveling overseas was "take twice the money and half the clothes". You only need to*

develop acute back pain and run out of cash near London's Piccadilly Circus to realize how pertinent that concept is.

Jet-lag is another entity which cannot be discounted. To state this another way, "long distance travel usually results in rapid transmeridian changes with consequent desynchronization of circadian rhythms.' Got that? Do not expect to be exceptionally perky the first day of your tour.

Have hard currency in your secure wallet for the country in which you are about to land. The equivalent of $150 will get you to a hotel and possibly a decent lunch.

If it is possible, keep your luggage quota to one checked bag and an allowable carry-on. Airline fees are a great motivating factor in this regard. Pack clothes as tightly and carefully as possible. One does not have to look/walk like a fashion model tramping through ancient sites and river routes. Comfortable, not easily soiled outfits need to be considered priorities. Better still are garments that are manufactured with fabric that has wrinkles purposely in the design.

Forget the lacy lingerie. Most people sleep without it anyway. Of course, I am not speaking from personal experience. A friend told me that juicy bit. A T-shirt can do double duty in a variety of ways.

There are a couple of articles which need to be packed in the over-the-shoulder purse. Depending on where you "go"-- pun intended --hand sanitizer is a must for swiping hands clean. In addition keep a small package of Kleenex within reach when you stop at a place that has facilities but no amenities. Do you know what I mean?

A thoughtful addition to any meal is a package of dried fruit, preferably of the plum variety. Many travelers are afflicted with a condition that is the opposite of the Aztec two-step.

A pocket-sized flashlight is another good entity to include. It is handy for reading maps at night or scoping unfamiliar bedrooms/bathrooms during an unexpected power outage.

Always include an umbrella. Always. For shade or precipitation.

Really clever tourists tuck in a foldable extra bag. It is utterly inconvenient to be compelled to purchase extra luggage to accommodate the scintillating articles we want to decorate our house or ourselves once the trip is history. Storage areas tell the tale of redundant suitcases.

Don't forget a small pack of emergency supplies. Do you know how to "mime" nausea in the middle of the Sahara? Around the clock drugstores are difficult to find if you are overcome with an allergy, sinusitis or fever. Besides if you are not fluent in Cantonese or Spanish, an error could be made which could prove to be ...grave. Include ASA or Tylenol, throat lozenges, hay fever tablets, bandaids, itch ointment plus anything else you may need. Hopefully the supply will never be used, but just in case, you are covered.

Wear a Canadian flag pin in your lapel or buy a camera strap with bright maple leaves on it. Something, anything to identify yourself as a Canadian. And be polite! If something bugs you, shut your mouth and think of the majestic Rockies. It is important to role model good manners to the rest of the world that is struggling with high political anxiety. Remember, our country is loved world wide.

A journal is an essential item for a number of reasons. Tidbits of information relating to customs, social interactions, cautionary notes re: weather, geography etc. I do not have a photographic memory so journal jottings afford the pleasures of traveling months later sitting by a roaring fire at the home place.

Without my recording the exchange between a dour Bed and Breakfast hostess in Scotland, I might have forgotten the underlying humour. Breakfast was a plate of kippers and blood sausage---we had a choice. I chose the kippers even though a couple of slices of Canadian back bacon would have been more favorable. When I requested kippers, she stared at me over her glasses and declared, *"I canna talk to you. Your accent is too strong!"* She refused to speak to me the entire time we stayed there focusing on Douglas who obviously had an accent she understood perfectly!

Two days after we flew out of Santiago, Chile a devastating earthquake brought ruin to some of the places we had visited shortly before. Reviewing my observations helped me understand how dreadful and frightening the situation was for the citizens who had escaped injury and death. A cruise to Norway was a lovely reminder of my adoptive mothers love of raspberries and sour cream.

A memorable 24 hours on a cruise around South America is worth forgetting! Approaching the Falkland Islands an unseasonable storm suddenly invaded our peaceful voyage. The towering waves forced the closure of all the decks. Our meals were made merry by crashing glasses and spilled drinks. After a while, no one was eating anything!! I felt miffed to spend several hours contemplating the ceramic features of a regulation-sized nautical toilet bowl. Naturally this too passed, but in ways I do not care to share.

A medical emergency added to the tension. A lively 83 year old woman was learning a new dance step at the height of the storm. She missed a beat, fell and fractured her left leg. A small boat arrived from Port Stanley onto which she was carefully hoisted through the cargo door. Lesson learned---do not try anything new when the ship is heaving through heavy waters.

Reading an entry from a quick trip to Israel made me grateful for the minor traffic jams we experience close to home. Tel Aviv is not known for graceful traffic. Major road construction has a way of encouraging the growth of patience. A truck stopped in front of our bus, the driver hopped out, raced over to a nearby cafe, bought himself a coffee and dashed back to his vehicle just in time to move it into the slow flow of traffic.

A walk through a cemetery is one of my favorite things to do. Fascinating in a non-morbid manner, the gravestones of people past their time helps me to focus on how quickly this present state is passing. Kenneth and I ambled through an ivy and thorn-laced graveyard of an adjoining slate-covered Church of Ireland. Most of the headstones were dated in the eighteenth century. Mold had splintered the surfaces making the original engraving difficult, if not impossible to decipher. Scratching a superficial layer of moss away from the chiseled lettering of one ancient tomb, I read this epitaph of a gentleman who died 2 decades before my adoptive father was born-" *Commemorate me with your life".* In other words, honour my life by living yours fully. A beautiful sentiment which speaks 2 centuries later.

Guiding a small foreign car around unfamiliar curves and hills always feels like an escapade from an Oscar-winning movie. So many sights at which to gaze and never enough hours. I thought about our Alberta Health Care Services when we passed a health care center with a *mortuary* attached to one side of it. How desperate are patients when they sign into that establishment?

Handel's *Messiah* has always clutched my heart to make Christmas or Easter really the religious observances they represent. The tipping factor is the first performance was in Dublin, Ireland, April 13, 1712. If a live concert is not a viable option, an excellent DVD is an acceptable substitute. I purchased a DVD that commemorates the 250th anniversary of the initial presentation in the same church as it was performed. Every December I treat myself to a private audition with earphones in place and a cuppa of Irish tea in hand. The most moving concert I attended was in Shanghai, China in 2005. Annually a assemblage of ex-pats gives a stirring rendition of this classic. Professors, missionaries, business people, and others all lend their talents in a shout out of God's goodness in this country which does not favour Christianity. Only foreigners are allowed to attend. One has to show their passport to prove that. Conversation in the small theater venue must not include any negative suggestions regarding government policies or restrictions. We were warned about the presence of spies sitting incognito in the audience. The evening was dubbed Handel's Music —not "The Messiah".

Every member of the audience stood, as tradition warrants, during the triumphant rendering of *The Hallelujah Chorus*. As I sat down I thought, *"Yes, Mr. President, you have tried to crush Christ out of your country, but in spite of your godless stance, the name of God has just been heard, loud and clear!"*

Kenneth fulfilled a life-long dream to place his feet on each of the 7 continents before he left this world in a permanent fashion. In January of 2014 he flew to Antarctica for an adventure like no other. Me? I enjoy Alberta's winter, but the trip promised no thrills to tantalize my imagination. To his credit and my delight, he faithfully kept a detailed account daily in a small striped journal. When I read the entries I felt I had been by his side. He captured the beauty of the sea surrounded by icebergs on his Sony camera. Later I endeavoured to reproduce the images in watercolour paintings. My meager effort helped me appreciate another part of this planet.

Two days after his arrival home, I conducted a seminar on Midlife Spirituality for a group of seven interested folks. Originally it was scheduled to be a church sponsored session, but due to low registration we decided to hold it at AL-VI-NOR. Determining a change in venue proved the correctness of the dateless axiom, *"God is in the details".* The openness of those in attendance combined with the non-judgmental listening to brutal truths rarely spoken in public proved to be life-changing for those gathered around a beckoning fireplace.

To expedite the refreshments and lunch, my friend Catherine Janke gave me her assistance and allowed me to be fully present with the ongoing discussions. As she was ascending the front steps with a lovingly made layer cake, she stumbled. The container flew from her hands and landed right-side up (thankfully) but at an odd angle which did nothing to improve her careful handiwork. The custard filling melded with the chocolate icing in an interesting pattern. We all agreed the presentation was still edible in spite of her moans and our commiserating chuckles. I turned the incident into a perfect metaphor for midlife living. All our dreams and meticulous planning can be demolished in a splinter of time without our permission. The Spirit of God hallowed the living room. More was accomplished in 6 hours than perhaps in 6 months of counseling.

Turning my grief experiences into something tangible meant nothing was wasted. Sleepless nights, tears, shredded plans, all yielded valuable building material to construct the frameworks of a new normal. I translated the anxiety of sorrows into "made by VRL" seminars. Further Education offices, schools, specialty groups and churches wanted to hear about navigating the grief process. No one else was engaged full time at a reasonable price so the opportunities were all mine. AL-VI-NOR became the preferred venue for day long sessions on *Aging and Spirituality, Art and Spirituality, Christmas Coping, Advent and Lent retreats and Days of Quiet.* Sharing these subjects with attendees who were eager to learn and share their own experiences was a joy that convinced me I would do this as long as I had strength and breath.

I was approached by the Sylvan Lake Ministerial to design an 8 week grief program for the community under their auspices. The town experienced a cluster of tragedies which undermined our sense of safety and the ability to cope with "urban center crime". We held a preliminary information session and 26 people attended! Accordingly, a plan was developed which served the community at large until 2016. Memorial Presbyterian Church offered their facilities as a meeting place as well as volunteers to help set up the seating arrangements and refreshments. I will always be grateful for the gracious assistance which aided the success of the evenings.

Often grief-stricken people manage their sorrow quite well if they have some kind of support—church fellowship, community connections and attentive family or friends. However, there are times when an individual's life has been turned into a mish-mash of further woe by hassling from family members who are walking a decidedly different path of recovery. Listening to countless tales of heart pain made me grateful for my own circumstances. I voluntarily relinquished *"The Mourning After"* following quiet reflection on a number of levels. I fully intended to continue the one day programs, which are similar to a concentrated dose of help in palatable form. The shorter sessions accommodate those unable to commit for an 8-13 week period. However, it was not to be at this time. An announcement in a church bulletin stated the date of a forthcoming new grief program to be introduced. That stung, as I had just chatted with the church leaders about another day session. Time lends a dusky covering over disappointments if we allow it. I now view the decision by someone else to sideline that part of my inventory was only a pause in which I could reevaluate what I really wanted to accomplish.

Fewer opportunities for seminars has opened up space for artistic creativity. As an emerging artist I find myself dabbling whenever I can with brush, paint and quality paper. Landscapes are out of my talent range. The price of Hallmark cards are out of my budget range. Painting celebration greetings or messages of solace now gives me an imaginative way to express myself.

The multifaceted life of a female parent leaves little time or energy to meditate on the splendid status which becomes a *good mother-in-law*. The main ache is to get the kids to grow up as God-fearing, polite, engaged citizens. Forget the minute details of a wedding and pray the marriage will exceed all expectations.

An addendum to that petition was *"Help me to be a lovable mother-in-law, please"*. Let's tell the truth. Women designated as such have a huge amount of bad press to suppress. When Rael and Leanne married late in the summer of 1992, 8 grandparents were alive and present. One by one they finished their earthly journey. The picture we have of them as a group is now beyond repeating. Regan and Tracey met on a blind date, something my mother warned me about! After the wedding in Red Deer, they settled in Sylvan Lake.

Things took a marvellous turn for the better when Renard met MaryJo Husker, born and raised in Wisconsin, U.S.A. They courted for sometime before they decided marriage was in their future. The wedding took place in Reedsburg, Wisconsin less than 2 months after the twin towers fell and changed the world's landscape. Traveling by air became a tournament between patience and anxiety in which no real winner was ever declared.

Their house began to expand with the arrival of Bronson Jesse in 2004.. Gavin Stewart followed 2 years later. Austyn Hope Ruth added a feminine touch later in 2008. Not to be left out of this growing family Robyn Meredith blessed us with her presence on April 11 two years later. A heart of love has the spectacular ability to expand to include"more". And when Dawson Wyatt Nathanial announced his arrival with a squeal in 2012 we knew without a doubt the truth of that exhortation. We were in the Calgary Airport enroute to London when I heard the soft "tap a tap" of his tiny pre-born heart. MaryJo had recorded it on her phone a few hours before I called when she was at the doctor's office.

The ecstasy of welcoming and enfolding these 5 "grandies" into the Lynn family circle was splintered by some health events as the decade drew to a close.

The "official" explanation of health was defined in 1948 by the World Health Organization as a "state of physical, mental and social well-being , not just the absence of disease." It included the capacity to maintain one's integrity and equilibrium. An updated and now preferred view is the ability to adapt and self-manage in the face of social, physical and emotional challenges. A grateful nod is owed to Dr. Machtela Huber for a worthy viewpoint. On a personal level, both aspects resonate. I will admit to rock-bottom moments when I seriously wondered if my ancestral DNA was attached somehow to a Hebrew guy named Job.

In October 2008 life was proceeding smoothly. Nothing on the surface was an indication that an insidious course of events was about to unfold. Marching into my family physician's examine room, I felt perky. Stumbling out 30 minutes later, I felt pukey.

Dr. Radomsky; *You look very pale!*
Virginia: *Really? I feel fine.*
Dr. Radomsky: *Have you lost weight lately?*
Virginia: *Well, not too much. Been doing the yard work and that is great exercise.*

> Dr. Radomsky: *I'm sending you for a STAT blood test. No one loses weight without trying.*
>
> Virginia: *Really? I do not have any symptoms—no pain, no nausea, nothing!*

A few moments later as she skillfully palpated my abdomen, she frowned. A shiver closed in and refused to let go. She informed me a CAT scan would be prudent decision. SHEESH! According to protocol things began to move quickly and I was booked for urgent surgery. My hemoglobin registered at 80—no wonder I was pallid! Surgery was successful and the pathology report decreed a lesion of the non-Hodgkin's variety was the culprit. A small bladder resection was necessary due to the aggressive growth since the initial CAT scan. The good news was the fact this particular cell type responds very well to chemotherapy.

My first few days at home post-op were uneventful. However at the end of the week I began to have unremitting pain in my lower left abdomen. Analgesics were abundantly unhelpful as my angst rose mountain high. We called an ambulance to expedite the ride back to the hospital. Once there, a CAT scan revealed a large abscess. A series of treatments were forthcoming and I survived another week on the surgical floor. Sleeping in my own bed with favorite foods on hand was a tremendous boon for the energy I needed to face the coming months. There were days when I inwardly whined *"First a tumor, now an abscess. What next, a clot?"* Should have fastened a clasp to my lips!

I prepared myself as best I could for a series of treatments I had prayed would never be mine to embrace. After overcoming initial resistance from the consultant assigned to my case, arrangements were made for the therapy to be given at the Cross Institute in Edmonton. This was a warm comfort as I was already familiar with the layout and expectations of the various care areas. A few days before the initial treatment, my friend Elizabeth Thain dropped by for tea bringing with her solace as well as a prayer shawl. She had handcrafted a knitted shawl with the softest wool imaginable. At the end of each row, she said a prayer for me. It was presented with such love and tenderness I just KNEW I was going to survive , even thrive, after all the consults and chemotherapy were finished 6 months down the road.

Stepping into the treatment suite that first Friday was a calm-wrecker. The nurse assigned to me was understanding and kind. It was the end of her first week in the treatment area. After 3 attempts to find a vein (and I am blessed with obvious ones), she called a colleague who was celebrating Chinese New Year. The young woman spotted a "willing" vein and in went the needle, no sweat. I wrapped the shawl around my shoulders and slid into a drowsy rest induced by the pre-drug regime administered before the IV cocktail of anti-cancer medications begins to flow.

Three weeks passed before my hair began to shed itself in clumps. The morning I woke up with knot of hair in my mouth was the day the decision was made to shave my head. My sister-in-law Jillian drove up from southern Alberta and did the deed a few days later. We devised a small ritual that helped ease the transition to baldness. Afterwards she told me I looked like a Buddhist nun! It was a suitable descriptor. The next day Rael with the spirit of devotion, underwent his own head shave. In a perverse sort of fashion, it was a frolic to be rid of bad hair days for 7 months. In addition it provided a wonderful excuse to purchase jaunty hats I otherwise would have passed by. No money had to be budgeted for haircuts or shampoo as the head that looked back at me from the mirror always looked the same. As a small measure of defiance against the meanness of the disease, I wore a rose tattoo (stuck on, NOT stuck in!!) on the crown of my head. Why not celebrate uniqueness?

During the time at the Cross Institute I noticed many sad, lonely patients. Often I would assign my guardian angel and her helpers to a specific person who seemed especially terror stricken or depressed. Praying for others had a calming affect on my heart rate and respirations.

A program entitled "Tapestry" was offered for a number of years at

KingsFold Retreat Center. The week long schedule included massage, counseling sessions, group discussions, music and art therapy for post-treatment cancer patients. A entire range of prognoses were represented. Two of the participants had already registered for hospice care. Unfortunately the current provincial government has rescinded funding and this valuable oasis of comfort is no longer available. Lamentable loss.

Spring came and left the door open for a wonderful summer. A celebration seemed reasonable in light of my returning health and energy level. We booked a cruise from Quebec to New York in late June. A day stopover in Halifax gave us a wonderful visit with Dorothy Mae, Kenneth's older sister.

Winter months were punctuated with Texas sunshine. I spent time with my husband in Huffman, a small town northeast of Houston. In March of 2011 I had a strange dream. Nighttime slumber is rarely nuanced by dreams of my deceased loved ones. One Sunday afternoon I needed a "horizontal pause". I was suddenly sitting with my mother (Alice) chatting about incidentals. She placed her arm on my tummy and asked, *"Are you okay, dear?"* Sure, I replied as I stroked her smooth hand, its frailness exactly the same as I remembered it. I awoke with a sense of fright to discover I was caressing my left arm which was positioned over my abdomen. The strange moment spun me into full consciousness when I realized I had no sensation in my arm. I rolled over and promptly fell off the bed. Unable to communicate with Kenneth by talking for a few moments, I finally convinced him to call an ambulance. I knew I had fallen victim to a stroke. In addition to the unfamiliar symptoms of speech my left arm was swinging around uncontrollably. Later I learned the name of this peculiar condition--- alien arm or alien limb syndrome. The medical explanation refers to it as "involuntary motor activity with a feeling of estrangement from the affected limb." Weird comes up hopelessly short in describing this phenomenon. The ambulance attendant strapped my left arm down because I kept unintentionally hitting him! I was encouraged to wear 2 pound weights on my arm in order to "tract" its movements.

Thankfully within 36 hours the distressing symptoms began to abate and then completely disappear.

The care I received at the Hermann Memorial Hospital was excellent. Travel insurance covered every last dollar which mitigated anxiety and no doubt hastened my recovery. I flew home the following weekend, welcomed by my family who were worried about my future, as well as theirs. I could walk, talk, and think coherently, but found putting on gloves, panty hose, inserting earrings, and picking up small objects tested my patience as well as my expectations for a full recovery. Everything can be managed. The "activities of daily living" were a great incentive for rehab at home. Except for diminished sensitivity in the soles of my feet and fingers, nothing remains to cue a reminder of the episode. A grateful heart is a daily offering to divine Providence.

The church we have attended for years in Kingwood, Texas underwent a colossal stroke of its own when our beloved pastor decided to return to his Jewish roots and denounce the basics of his ministry's teaching. Confusion and "alien limbs" were the order of the day for months. It was difficult to worship in an atmosphere of lost trust. Slowly the congregation has regained a state of stability and we are moving on. Ratched-up hearts need a great deal of healing before full function is regained. So many questions, so many unanswered queries.

My bucket list is rather sparse these days. The majority of items are now obsolete. Newfoundland? You bet---been there twice. The first time at the end of a hurricane. Lake LaRonge in northern Saskatchewan? Yes. Departure a month earlier would have been beneficial, but still the memories of nature's bounty remain vivid. Holland in tulip time? Don't think I'll make it this time around. A trip down the Pacific Coast Highway? It took a long time to percolate, but finally in 2011 we did it. Driving a safe distance from the edge of the highway on the seaside was not an option due to the meager road allowance. Good idea to assure any cardiac or hypertension medications have been swallowed and absorbed before glancing down at the yawning cliffs and billowing ocean waves collaborating how to eat the car once it toppled over the banks. The trip straightened my hair—for free.

Remember I mentioned the importance of a pro-active visit to a family doctor yearly exam? Late in October 2013 I made a trek into the nearest city for a mammogram. A call back appointment was recommended. My nerves started playing hopscotch as a biopsy was scheduled at the Cross Institute. The results arrived 2 days before Christmas. Human error delayed the immediate reporting of the results which caused high grade anxiety. Perhaps it was willful neglect? Let me not be judgmental, oh Lord. Rael, Leanne and family arrived to celebrate the season in Texas just hours after the biopsy report arrived via Email. By a huge measure of grace I was able to compartmentalize the news and fully enjoy the vacation with them. The usual appointments and consults were waiting for me when I flew back in the New Year. Early in February I had a lumpectomy which was without incident. I said my farewell to my complete left breast in a wee ritual that assured me this was life, and I was alive and this was only an uncivil interruption to my nicely planned springtime calendar. A 3 week course of radiation followed at the Cross (where else??). The team of radiologists agreed on a certain protocol which enjoyed a 95% non-recurrence rate. How could I refuse when I had so much yet to accomplish? I stayed at Sorrentino's House, a refuge for women undergoing cancer treatment at the Cross Institute. It is supported by the generosity of a family that had to abide the savagery of a cancer invasion.

The state of my spirit was a shade lighter than indigo as we approached the entrance. I felt so vulnerable. This well-appointed dwelling near the treatment center has room for 14 women. The common areas provide a healing atmosphere of camaraderie while the kitchen facilities bring up dreams of home improvement. Cob's Bakery brings in baking goods every day; Second Cup Coffee Co. provides excellent coffee. A quilting club in Camrose, Alberta gifts each guest with a quilt for them to enjoy during their stay and then at home. MaryJo accompanied me as I settled in and adjusted to my reality.

Patients are driven by volunteers to the various areas of treatment daily, except on weekends. The drivers are cancer survivors who understand the anxiety which coexists with the diagnosis. Every autumn a fund-raising gala is held to raise awareness of Sorrentino House as well as garner monetary support to make its operation possible. "Fashion With Compassion" was the theme the following October. I was asked to be a model representing women who were alumni of Sorrentino House. Seven other ladies, some who had been guests during the same time as myself, also were chosen. For 2 days we were treated like royals! Fashions for men, women and children were featured from a variety of local retail establishments. It was an eyeopener to catch a glimpse of the other side of modeling! I made a decision to purchase the dress I chose for the occasion. It has been worn several times since and always serves as lovely excuse to manage a ticket for a cruise!!

Grandchildren have the propensity to enter high school and begin to sprinkle their conversations with choosing careers, saving money to purchase a means of conveyance without bothering their parents for every needed excursion. In addition, sometimes a beau or special girl is added to the mix and life for everyone is hoisted up a notch.

Nothing on my "real time" horizon was indicative of an indistinct cloud making its way closer to our nicely planned Christmas activities. The usual appointment for my annual medical exam was made as I thought about decorating the house and buying stocking stuffers in weather that was kinder than Alberta's. Dr. Hyde took an inordinate amount of time palpating the right side of my abdomen. Finally she said, *"I feel something on your liver. I will order an MRI to verify whatever this is".*

"Something on your liver"---absolutely the most terror-riven words I wanted to hear due to my past history of surgeries. The scan was integral for a proper diagnosis and future treatment. I was asymptomatic—no weight loss, discomfort or digestive irregularities. The day she received the scan report she phoned. It was a Friday. Yes, there was a large lesion present, but it lacked the typical configuration of carcinoma, although the possibility of cancer could not be ruled out entirely at the time.

I was not interested in having a tete-a-tete chat with the Lord of the universe that evening. I have to be honest. Whining isn't pretty. I sat in the living room listening to the fireplace have a conversation with itself. The crackling flames and glowing embers tempered my mood somewhat. My thoughts centered on Kenneth and my sons and their families. Another valley to traverse, as if they didn't have enough hassles of their own. The following Monday morning we saw Dr. Hyde in her Red Deer clinic. Once again we were launched into a now familiar schedule of further testing, consults with specialists, pre-op meetings with the admission nurse and anesthesiologist. On January 3, 2017 a lesion, the size of a small football, was excised from my liver. We waited 3 weeks for the pathology report to assure us no cancerous cells were found in the specimen. The rogue cyst was filled with blood. Well, yahoo for that! Hallelujahs were loud and clear as we reflected on our blessings. Support from family and friends lent an incredible atmosphere in which to heal post-op. I gained further insight into the importance of being kind to oneself as the delicate process of muscles re-knitting themselves into wholeness and strength takes place .

Surgical protocols and the regimes that precede them and immediately following, have been modified to improve the experience for the patient. The majority of surgical procedures do not require an 8-12 hour fasting period. Someone facing an operation is now allowed a drink of water up to 4 hours previous. Such a boon psychologically as well as physically. A "diet as tolerated" is encouraged as soon as the patient feels hungry. No more insipid broth which has been diluted for the sake of economics or watery porridge without the enhancement of salt. After five days of malnourishment due to a combo of nausea, hunger and discomfort, I asked my surgeon's colleague as he made ward rounds, if I could have Booster Juice. He replied," *Of course you can! I will write it in the orders."* Within the hour I had my wish fulfilled. Rejuvenation was immediate and phenomenal. That evening I enjoyed roast pork, gravy, potatoes, salad and dessert without adverse

A Portrait in Progress

reactions. Something to keep in mind for future reference.

The variety of pigments available allows the artist a wide range of nuances enabling richer uniqueness and beauty of the finished work, Red, blue, yellow, brown. black, even white—all have the ability to be blended by a clean brush into subdued edges which stand in contrast with crisp texturing. I have come to appreciate all eventualities have the purpose of softening the surround of my heart. This perceptiveness alleviates the urge for relentless agitation.

The Frame: Summation and Perspective

I SUPPOSE IF someone chose to give my life a cursory examination could comment it has been one marry adventure after another. When the laughter died away, who could fault them?

Winston Churchill once commented "The longer you look back the farther you can look ahead." The world thanks him for this nugget of wisdom. This memoir has involved a process of looking back. Reading hundreds of pages-—diaries, journals and letters-- precipitated long lost memories with all the emotional packaging. I was caught unaware at some of the elements I have taken for granted. It was a pleasure to reacquaint myself with the antics of my youngsters as fatigue in those early years of childrearing erased much of my recall of that era. Reviewing the discomfort of my losses brought unexpected malaise and moments of sheer dread.

The painting of my life, meticulously designed and implemented by the Divine master painter, has been graphically enhanced by a multitude of events as well as my response to them. Basically I remain the young woman, holding in her heart love and more to share, energized by dreams within her potential grasp. The tendency to harbour a naive worldview has been replaced with clear-headed thinking fringed with a touch of brass.

Clinical Pastoral Education helped me move past self-imposed limitations nourished and adorned by being a woman, a nurse and a clergywife. I cannot escape the existential angst (is that not a delightful term?!) which comes from being spread-eagled between the comfort of the past and the freshness of the future. I have learned to claim my own authority without being slathered into guilt by backtracking and second guessing my intuitive self. Dealing with people in crisis situations within an institutional milieu taught me to ask *"Whose event/issue is this? Mine or theirs?"* That in-house education has proved beneficial in many situations.

My early spiritual formation was activated in an evangelical subculture where one is considered a "good parent" if one's adult children attend some variety of church. The prevailing posturing is *"Ya followed all da rules".* I no longer buy into that area of thought. It has a pernicious way of engendering guilt in some parents while inspiring nose-thumbing pride in the hearts of others whose children haven't broken rank. Yet. I have come a long way in the understanding of crafting a portrait. Painting instruments in the hand of the Master Painter can be compared to eventualities in the lives of family members also as their picture of life is completed one brush stroke at a time. I have unshakable faith in all my children (genetically-tied as well as step) that their hearts and lives will be guided by the Holy Spirit.

When it was my privilege to work as a pastoral personage in a hospital setting I found it helpful to view my chaplaincy as a way of drawing science and spirituality together. Both those entities are on opposite sides of a chasm. The chaplain stands in the middle, on a bridge so to speak, and endeavours to draw them closer in a meaningful way. The path is strewn with failures, victories and a whole lot of laughter mingled with a bounty of tears.

Out of necessity I have revisited my own personal perceptions of Virginia. Old thought patterns/habits die slowly and give out agonizing groans as they expire!! New freedom to express opinions assertively in an arena where fresh thinking is sometimes viewed with squint-eyed paranoia is now firmly in my survival cache.

The nuances in the portrait of my life lend a sense of absurdity when viewed from any perspective. Who else in my acquaintanceship has 3 of her "home born" sons, 5 stepchildren and 20 grandchildren? I will admit of course, not all are within hugging distance. I cannot name another woman who has seen London, England 3 times, each occasion accompanied by a different husband. I remember a quote that is attributed to Goethe which states, " *We are shaped by those we love.*" I rest my case.

I continue to wrestle with and modify my beliefs about suffering. Friedrich Nietzsche said,*"That which does not destroy me, makes me stronger."* Most days that is true, but sometimes the last word needs to be ...*stranger!* Ernest Hemingway expressed it another way," *The world breaks everybody, but some people become strong at the broken places."* I have used that quote in my seminars since 1980,

My pastoral identity often comes up for review. I have a deep conviction I am "called" to rural Alberta at this time. The "Messiah Complex" which had residency in my life for an extended length of time has suffered a mortal blow. I cannot "fix" everything for everybody. The truth is, I could never perform that kind of magic in the past either. I have to allow, even encourage, folks to pick up the consequences of unwise decisions or judgment calls, ascertain the lesson and move into greater wholeness. No one fixed anything for me. As a result I am wiser, stronger and own plenty of resilience. Looking back in quiet reflection I can see I was "ahead of my time" when I planned and taught stress management, bereavement preparation and recovery as well as end of life issues. Successfully organizing AL-VI-NOR into a healing entity without a model to follow has been a hallmark of accomplishment.

When I am in the throes of an indistinct, possibly murky even, predicament I am blessed with irrefutable reminders of God's faithfulness. How can I express the emotion I felt when motoring through Edmonton at rush hour, I heard my name announced on CBC? Driving home after receiving devastating news I turned the car radio to dilute my despair. Less than 10 seconds passed before I heard I was the first place winner of a postcard contest. I had forgotten I had entered, but at the precise moment I needed some assurance of divine care, it was delivered to me. A sequel of laughter to tears! The secure knowledge of my "calling" allows me the liberty of self-affirmation. Naturally, it is a lovely thing if others occasionally do that, but the lack thereof does not constitute an irreparable crisis of psyche.

A portion of scripture written by the prophet Isaiah and echoed in Matthew 12, verse 20 talks about Christ's deportment as he began his ministry...."*He won't yell, cause a commotion, won't walk over anyone's feelings, won't push you into a corner..*" This is "The Message" in contemporary language. The ancient prophet saw the Messiah as one who could address the issues without crushing the spirit of those broken and contrite. Christ emphasized the spiritual aspects of his Kingdom without engaging in public haranguing or unsavory politicking. This seems, in an oblique fashion, to describe my desired pastoral identity and presence.

The wise writer of Proverbs knew about life when he wrote *"unrelenting disappointment leaves you heartsick. But a sudden good break can turn life around."* Again, a nugget from "The Message". I can assist my clients and friends to re-frame their circumstances in light of the Divine. People who are fried by situations not of their making or exasperated by the mechanics of living, can be resuscitated by breathing in the Presence of the Almighty and allowing the greater wisdom to overtake their inadequacies.

My resilience speaks to the actuality there IS life after crushing disappointment and loss. Sometimes in the ashes of ruined hope, delightful surprises are found. Not always immediately or without attentiveness, of course. There is a difference between the *reason* for an illness or brokenness and the *meaning* of the experience.

Many years ago I heard the Anglican Bishop Victoria Matthews relate the story of a piece of artwork in one of her Ontario parishes. The artist (I regret his/her name escapes me) designed a crucifix with the cross fashioned from rough, unhewn wood. The body of Christ was cleverly made of mirrors. A person gazing on the work of art can literally see themselves in the body of Christ. Most of the time

The Frame: Summation and Perspective

this visual representation has a profound effect on the person. On one level I can easily visualize myself reflecting the work of Christ in my community, my circle of influence. I have a responsibility to be a change agent wherever, whenever I am able.

The landscape of my own losses gives me a window into many similar situations in the lives of others. Using the imagery of reflection once again, this acts as a mirror of sorts. I see a bit of myself in everyone's trial.

A hearing impairment occasions times of humour as well as humiliation. One time I presented my passport, clearly open to the page which stated my Canadian citizenship. The immigration officer asked me a question. I assumed he was inquiring if I had brought any fruit into the country. That information was right in front of him also on the declaration form. I said, *"Yes sir, 6 lemons and 4 avocados."* He pushed his reading glasses down and said, *"I asked you what your citizenship was!"* Oh excuse me! I always believed reading comprehension was one of the requirements for that kind of a position. Oh well, gave me a giggle anyway.

Pastoral presence has broad connotations for me. I feel comfortable being a "minister" even though I am uncomfortable with the word. Opportunities for ministry exist everywhere. I am not constrained to a pulpit, an organization or even a bedside. I believe my background training and experiences serve as non-documented credentials which are valuable tools in this arena. Coupled with a secure inner direction, they give me the impetus I need to fulfill my place in a Divine scheme within the context of the body of Christ. My community (in a global sense) is my parish.

How many threads of connectedness do I have with my guests? Ahh-h, let me count the ways!

*Abandonment *Church hierarchy rigidity
*Adoption *Credential termination
*Cross-cultural living *Job loss
*Widowhood *Forgiveness process

>   *Blending families   *Serious health crises
>   *Meeting birth mother   *Hearing impairment
>   *Finding half-siblings   *Betrayal
>   ETCETERA!

And I might as well add, learning to have a friendly relationship with an ex-wife along with dealing with the memories of a wonderful deceased wife. Just a normal lifetime! I have come to view my job termination as a GIFT, fully understanding the best gifts in life are not often wrapped in silver and gold, adorned with remarkable ribbons. It took a catastrophic event to move me out into a place of freedom which required a different set of strengths. The situation reinforced my belief I was not created to be self-sustaining. As a result, I lean into the resources divinely provided for me with a sense of peace anchored with commitment.

I have moved along the pathway of healing/loss recovery in a fashion that is open to discussion. The entire sequence has not yet been revealed. Nevertheless, although I have healed, I certainly have not lost my memory. Some time ago I attended a session presided over by an executive officer who resembled Fabian Marshall. The resemblance was so striking I had difficulty absorbing his presentation.

One of my goals at this stage of life, is to live to be ninety..wits intact and mobility skills superb. An addendum to that, of course, is to age in place. Read that as *sage in place.* Every year that fades into history relinquishes its days to the succeeding 12 months. This convinces me if I persist in viewing all eventualities through a lens which sharply divides into black or white categories, severe visual headaches will be precipitated all the days of my life. Once in awhile, sipping on a cup of Chai tea and meandering in the memories, I ask this question to my innermost self, *"How have I become who I am on the basis of where I have been?"* These pages attempt to answer that in part.

I suppose the process has confirmed the will of God is *revealed,* not found.

In recent years I have released numerous comfort zones and

embraced possibilities instead. Life-givng, variegated, spine-tingling---all good!!! Plastic smiles that smothered internal strife and agonizing queries regarding Providential management in my life, had to be released completely. I need to personally wrestle into private actuality the conviction the "God Who Is There" really is. In a multitude of ways Lewis Adamic hit the nail on the head when he exclaimed, " *Life is like licking honey off a thorn".*

I have come to believe individuals are basically the same in the later stages of life as in youth years. Elemental personality traits remain. This comes from informal observation combined with 15 years of geriatric nursing. Embarking on this project has assisted me in observing myself, not necessarily with knives and daggers, but with a rather measured consideration. Does the aforementioned declaration hold true for me at this present time? What areas do I need to fine tune?

The following article was written shortly after my second widowhood. It was published as one of my weekly "Lynnsight" columns.

> *Individuals make a hideous mistake if they attach themselves to the concept that if an elusive goal is finally attained, grasping its triumph will bring them everlasting satisfaction and happiness.*
>
> *Far safer and beneficial is the view that life is not merely a destination. The entire route is fascinating because of the innumerable side-steps each bringing with it an appropriate quota of ecstasy, disappointment, sorrow and hope. It is a rare good buddy who feels and proves it by previous experience, his/her life is glitch free. Not one of my acquaintances dare boast they possess infallibility in the area of judgment calls.*
>
> *The very fact life tends to be rather uneven lends strength to the development of one's "inner core". Women and men who run with and learn from actually living through events viewed either as negative or positive, generally have a great*

A Portrait in Progress

deal to offer others. They resist the temptation to whine or openly brag over what has happened.

Robert Schuller authored a book entitled "Life's Not Fair, But God is Good". It is a non-preachy type of treatise. No one points a finger to lay charges or breathes down thunder and judgment pronouncements that begin with "you should have" and end with "next time do it better". All such exhortations are designed of course to produce a feeling of guilt along with a sense of unworthiness.

Robbie Burns had a shaft of inspiration nearly 2 centuries ago when he wrote " The best laid plans of mice and men often go astray". Meticulous planning, careful execution of strategy, all warmed in the oven of prayer if you wish, do not combine to guarantee perfect consequences. Mind you, those previously named activities help to lessen the regrets and personal sorrow which are sure to follow a perceived failure.

Pristine ability to see the future clearly is still a far-off hope for most of us. In the meantime, frequent reality checks will keep us close to the path as possible.

Sure there are questions when things don't work out as planned. Lots of them, and a good number of them unanswerable. A person is in trouble if the basis for rebuilding their life depends on totally understanding all the negative circumstances or events in their life.

I am acutely aware the process of blending families is energy-expending, time consuming and occasionally, financially depleting. The operative phrase, if the whole exercise is to become successful, is "flexible overcompensation".

Every family has its own style of communicating which lay in darkened closets undetected by a newcomer. Those areas are never ventured into, even by an ardent conversationalist. Value systems possess great variances. Often an unintentional breach of some unknown code can spawn hurt and anger. It takes more than 3½ years to discover the recesses of a newly attached family group. Folks whose lives have been singularly linear can never quite "go there".

Celebrations are the sweet confections of life which break up the monotony of a regulated life. Norma and I celebrated our 76th year of living in a southern hotel that could boast of uninterrupted service for over a century. We walked along Galveston's beach sidewalk and ate a late evening meal on a wind strewn patio. I learned about great deals at "happy hour". In addition to that nugget, I found out that if a classy SPA includes a glass of bubbly prior to an appointment for a massage, one does need the services of a therapist!

Along this pathway called "living to the fullest" I have learned a few things . Unfortunately most of the learning requires repeat instruction before the lesson is fully absorbed. For example, I must find out for myself if something is good, bad or neutral, true or false. It can be perilous to decide completely on the basis of another's opinion. Of course I am not advocating a disregard of a studied opinion by a trusted individual who operates with good lateral thinking. Developing a fine tuned intuition has been a tremendous asset in navigating life's landscapes.

On an breezier precautionary note. Delete from a menu for 48 hours prior to any flight any items that contain beans (chili, Boston Brown legumes, four bean salad and so on). Their ability to produce intestinal rumbles has the possibility of providing a secondary airborne experience requiring the expertise of haz-mat connoisseurs!

To my descendants I want to encourage the value of observation skills. Develop the inner ecology of a master sleuth. Practice the art of defining body language. Memorize details- licence plates as well as facial features. Endear yourselves to others by recalling and using their names. Remember your smile can brighten someone else's face.

I take the long view of life. Cumulatively, I have lost nothing. No relationship, no position, no grief has been in vain. As I have assimilated the actualities of years past, I have structured them into the texture of my life-painting. An authentic life evolves over a span of many years. I want to be energized to make the latter part of my life exceed the expectations of the former.

Perhaps when my family members read this account they will feel affirmed regarding the abundant blessings the Lynns have enjoyed. Perhaps a detailed reflection of their mother's essence will lengthen horizons and grant them an understanding of this eternal, providential work of art, creatively designed on the canvass of one woman's humanity.

The frame, which ends up surrounding a finished portrait, must not be in competition for it in the area of design or beauty. A well-chosen frame adds a touch of completeness which incorporates the message the artist wished to convey. The more profound the thought, feeling and creativity an artist puts into her/his work, the more it unfolds to an alert spectator.

A portrait of significance is displayed on a wall where it can be readily studied. Perhaps a mirror can be positioned nearby to aid the observer in reflecting on their own "portrait in progress". A painting is created to inspire the viewer. This worthy expectation can also align itself to a life story.

The intricacies of an original painting (texture, colours, design details etc.) are by nature unique. No numbered prints or posters are allowed to lessen the inspiration. This memoir was written with reading in mind. One does not require celebrity status to make an impact.

> *Even the saddest things can become,*
> *once we have made peace with them,*
> *a source of wisdom and strength for the*
> *journey that still lies ahead.*
> Frederick Buechner, quoted in "A Grace Disguised"

CPSIA information can be obtained
at www.ICGtesting.com
Printed in the USA
LVOW12*2213230518
578277LV00001B/1/P